FAo

⊠ BABYLON, NEXT TO NINEVEH ⊠

BABYLON, NEXT TO NINEVEH

Where the World Began

EDWARD RICE

FOUR WINDS PRESS   NEW YORK

PHOTO CREDITS

British Museum, pp. 46, 48, 53, 55 (both), 63, 158, 162
John R. Freeman, 58
Constance Ftera, vi, 75
Jubilee, 172
Staatliche Museen Zu Berlin, 6
All other photographs by Edward Rice

LIBRARY OF CONGRESS CATALOGING IN PUBLICATION DATA

Rice, Edward
Babylon, next to Nineveh.

Includes index.
1. Near East—History. I. Title.
DS62.R45   935   79–12809
ISBN 0-590-07438-5

PUBLISHED BY FOUR WINDS PRESS
A DIVISION OF SCHOLASTIC MAGAZINES, INC., NEW YORK, N.Y.
COPYRIGHT © 1979 BY EDWARD RICE
ALL RIGHTS RESERVED
PRINTED IN THE UNITED STATES OF AMERICA
LIBRARY OF CONGRESS CATALOG CARD NUMBER: 79–12809
BOOK DESIGN BY CONSTANCE FTERA

1 2 3 4 5 83 82 81 80 79

CONTENTS

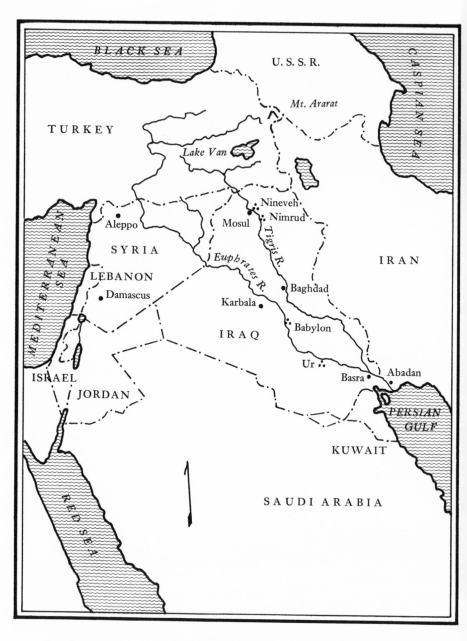

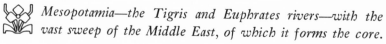
Mesopotamia—the Tigris and Euphrates rivers—with the vast sweep of the Middle East, of which it forms the core.

1

INTRODUCTION

A FRIEND ASKED ME WHAT THIS CURRENT WORK WAS ABOUT.
"Babylon," I said.
"Babylon, Long Island? That's a pretty limited subject."
"No," I replied, "Babylon, next to Nineveh."

This book is a personal selection of events that occurred in the great world of the Middle East that is centered along two of the most famous rivers of history—the Tigris and the Euphrates. The selection has to be personal and limited because it covers nearly six thousand years of recordable history and another six-to-twelve thousand years before that. One could write a hundred books about the area and barely skim the surface. So I write in terms of individuals and events, of the grand sweep highlighted by both the unusual and the typical.

The Tigris and the Euphrates flow through a land the ancient Greeks called "Mesopotamia"—land between the rivers. They are also part of a great arc known as the Fertile Crescent, which has produced fertile crops of both land and intellect. Not only were plants and animals first domesticated there, but it was the scene for the founding of the earliest towns and cities, as well as of civilization itself. We find in Mesopotamia all the attributes of a cultured, ordered life: laws, literature, schools, horticulture and agriculture, medicine, astronomy (and astrology), philosophy, education, and a thousand other things that enter into the development of the human race. It was in Mesopotamia that the most crucial, basic, and sensitive of all human techniques, the art of writing, was developed. (The Chinese discovered it independently only centuries later.) Because so many tons of ancient documents, in the form of clay tablets, sometimes multilingual, have survived, along with inscriptions on temple and palace walls and on the sides of cliffs, we possess much detailed information about Mesopotamian life in all its forms. We know of the original Sumerians and their successors and enemies—Akkadians, Babylonians, Assyrians, Hittites, Hurrians, Amoreans, and many other peoples; and we know much also about the later inhabitants of the Fertile Crescent—Persians, Arabs, Turks, and Europeans. From Mesopotamia came the first known codes of law, the first epic literature that was written down, the first maps. The tablets and inscriptions tell us about horticulture and agriculture, philosophy, social reform, education, concern for the poor and the aged, commerce and industry, kings, warriors, builders, and prophets. History began at Sumer, and even this book is a living proof, for it depends upon a variation of the old Sumerian alphabets for its own alphabet. Also the very handy, very important invention of paper, a Chinese discov-

*The land is often harsh, rocky and infertile, but alongside
the rivers and their tributaries, and now in newly found wells
dug by the United Nations, farmers are beginning to expand
the areas under cultivation.*

ery, was mostly a central Asian secret until Turkish traders
brought it to the Arabs. As the late inheritors of the Sumerians,
the Arabs then made it such a common object in the Middle
East that the Crusaders, impressed by its serviceability, brought
it home. So today these two seemingly simple discoveries have
become basic tools of the entire world. We will see other
Mesopotamian influences in the course of this book.

THE SEARCH FOR EVERLASTING LIFE

ALMOST FIVE THOUSAND YEARS AGO A GREAT HERO-KING BUILT the outer walls of the largest and most famous city then known. The city was Uruk; the Bible, which was written over two thousand years later, calls it Erech; today's maps identify it as Warka. The king was Gilgamesh, and while few people can place him now, in the ancient past in the Middle East he was one of the most famous of all kings, and perhaps the only one celebrated in poetry and song. In the last century, when archaeologists excavated Uruk's outer wall, they found that it ran five-and-a-half miles in length. Gilgamesh boasted that: "One third of [Uruk] is city, one third is garden, and one third is field, with the precincts of the goddess Ishtar." The great epic which recounts Gilgamesh's exploits says:

> In Uruk he built walls, a great rampart, and the temple of the blessed Eanna for the god of the firmament Anu, and for

4

Ishtar the goddess of love. Look at it still today; the outer wall where the cornice runs, it shines with the brilliance of copper; and the inner wall, it has no equal. Touch the threshold, it is ancient. Approach Eanna, the dwelling of Ishtar, our lady of love and war, the like of which no latter-day king, no man alive can equal. Climb upon the wall of Uruk; walk along it, I say; regard the foundation terrace and examine the masonry: Is it not burnt brick and good? The seven sages laid the foundation.

In his lifetime Gilgamesh was famous for his sexual appetites, wars, forcing his people to work on the wall, drafting the young men for his armies, and exploiting the populace—characteristics hardly unusual among kings and rulers of the past. But what makes Gilgamesh different is that he is the first figure in history whom we can see as an individual, as a man, though a partially mythologized one, rather than a deity. Gilgamesh loves and hates, weeps, rejoices, hopes, despairs, strives and wearies, and becomes more human and humane as the stories about him progress from the first tales, in which he is seen as a cruel, rapacious ruler, to those of the final episodes, which depict his search, fruitless as he suspects from the very beginning it will be, for immortality. Beset by doubts and fears, anxious to learn the secret of life everlasting, that secret which the gods retain for themselves alone, Gilgamesh is the epitome of man. He embodies man's worst and best characteristics—cruelty, anger, love, loyalty, ambition, greed, hope—but he knows always that, unlike the gods, he is mortal. He is a man of flesh and blood, and not a primitive deity descended to earth to drink and have affairs, fight, lie, and cheat, as the gods did in past times.

The awareness of man's fragility on earth came to Gilgamesh only slowly, and only upon the death of his great friend

Enkidu, his "brother." Enkidu is as interesting a figure as Gilgamesh, for he too represents one of the primordial forms of man's character and being, the man of innocence, of the wild, who is forcibly awakened into the world of civilization. Enkidu was "born," or created, because the gods were distressed not only by Gilgamesh's rapacity for forcing men into his armies and work gangs, but also for his attitude toward

A Sumerian cylinder seal shows Gilgamesh's companion Enkidu wrestling with two lions. This theme, with many variations, has been found through Mesopotamia and on stamp seals unearthed as far away as the Indus Valley on the Indian subcontinent.

women. The epic laments that: "His lust leaves no virgin to her lover, neither the warrior's daughter nor the wife of the noble." So the gods created Enkidu in the wilderness, out of clay (as *Adama*, man, was), and he lived like an animal. "He was innocent of mankind, he knew nothing of the cultivated land." Enkidu was primordial man in all his simplicity and goodness, eating grass with the gazelles and jostling at the water holes with the herds of wild game. He rescued the animals from the hunters' pits and filled them in. But such a life had to come to an end. One day a trapper came face-to-face with Enkidu at a water hole. Shivering with fear the trapper returned home, benumbed with terror by his encounter with the man of the wild.

With his livelihood at stake because Enkidu had been freeing the animals, the trapper visited Gilgamesh and asked his help. But he sought help in a very sophisticated way, not requesting soldiers to overpower the wild man but a woman to seduce him when he came down to the wells. "He will embrace her," pointed out the trapper, "and then the wild beasts will reject him." The trapper returned to the water hole with a prostitute, and there both waited for two days. On the third day the wild beasts came to drink, followed by Enkidu. The prostitute bared herself.

> She was not ashamed to take him; she made herself
> naked and welcomed his eagerness.
> She incited the savage to love
> And taught him the woman's art.

After six days and seven nights, having thoroughly lost his primordial innocence, Enkidu left the woman to return to his wild friends. When the animals saw him, they fled. Enkidu would have followed but:

his body was bound as though with a cord,
his knees gave way when he started to run,
his swiftness was gone.

The animals disappeared, for Enkidu had stepped over the boundary between the world of the wild and the world of civilization. His primal innocence gone, Enkidu became "man" in a most unpleasant sense.

Enkidu had grown weak, for wisdom was in him
and the thoughts of a man were in his heart.

The prostitute talked to him of the city, of Uruk, of the people there, of the temple of the goddess of love, of the great king, Gilgamesh, "who is very strong, and like a wild bull lords it over men." She spoke of the city in which every day was a holiday and the people dressed in gorgeous robes; the young men and the young women were wonderful to see. "How sweet they smell!" The woman persuaded Enkidu to leave the wilderness. But the full step into the city was yet beyond Enkidu. He moved to a village to live with shepherds. He turned against his wild friends, the animals, hunting down wolves and lions to protect the flocks of the civilized people. Finally, as the gods had planned, the people of Uruk called upon Enkidu to save them from Gilgamesh, who was planning to rape a young bride. Enkidu entered the city and went to the market place amid the cheers of the people and to the house where the bride was awaiting her husband and stood in the doorway. Gilgamesh came to take the bride. Enkidu barred the doorway, and the two men began to wrestle. They grappled, locked together like two bulls in battle. In their heroic struggle they broke the doorposts and the walls shook. On and on the struggle went, the two men each trying to throw the other. Then:

Gilgamesh bent his knee with his foot planted on
the ground, and with a turn Enkidu was thrown.
Immediately, then, his fury died.

Enkidu and Gilgamesh embraced to seal their friendship.
The king then abandoned his ferocious, lecherous ways. It was
a mutual taming: Enkidu became "civilized," and Gilgamesh
attained a measure of simplicity from his new friend and
brother. They embarked on a series of adventures, half-
mythological in character, but probably based on some kind
of fact, for in the old clay tablets which depict the epic there
are names and places, incidents which obviously originated
in actuality but which were romanticized and mythologized.

A crisis, a turning point, came when the goddess Ishtar, the
great Mesopotamian deity of love, made advances to Gilgamesh and he rejected her. Furious at being spurned Ishtar had
a formidable creature, the Bull of Heaven, created, which she
sent to earth to destroy Gilgamesh and his city. Hundreds of
Uruk's warriors lost their lives in the struggle before Enkidu
and Gilgamesh could kill the Bull. Then, in return for the loss
of the Bull, Ishtar demanded one more life, that of Enkidu.
He died of what seemed to be a fever, as Gilgamesh watched.
The ordeal had taken thirteen days. In mourning, a distraught
Gilgamesh sang one of the most beautiful dirges of epic literature. A few lines:

> Hear me, great ones of Uruk,
> I weep for Enkidu, my friend,
> Bitterly moaning like a woman mourning
> I weep for my brother.
> O Enkidu, the wild ass and the gazelle
> That were father and mother,
> All four-footed creatures who fed you
> Weep for you . . . .

Weep, all the paths where we walked together,
And the beasts we hunted, panther and tiger,
Lion and leopard, stag and ibex,
The bull and the doe.
The mountain we climbed where we slew the watchman
Weeps for you,
The river along whose bank we used to walk,
Weeps for you. . . .
The tillers and the harvesters
Who brought grain for you once
Mourn for you now.
The servants who anointed your body
Mourn for you now;
The harlot who anointed you with fragrant oil
Laments for you now;
The women of the palace, who brought you a wife
With the ring of your choice,
Lament for you now.

The last few lines show Gilgamesh's awakening awareness of the meaning of death.

An evil fate has robbed me.
O my young brother Enkidu, my dearest friend,
What is this sleep which holds you now?
You are lost in the dark and cannot hear me.

When Gilgamesh touched his friend's heart it did not beat, nor did Enkidu lift his eyes. Gilgamesh "began to rage like a lion" before Enkidu's body. Anguished and angry the king wandered in a daze about the great steppelands of Mesopotamia, mourning his friend. But he was also aware of something that struck him, too: his own mortality.

How can I rest, how can I be at peace?
Despair is in my heart.

What my brother is now, that shall I be
when I am dead.

"I am afraid of death," he said to himself. With this state-
ment ancient literature passed from the legendary to the fac-
tual, for we see Gilgamesh as mortal as any of us, not a divinity
or a hero mythologized beyond acceptance. "Afraid of death,"
Gilgamesh set out to search for the secret of everlasting life,
for the secret that the gods keep to themselves. In all of mankind there was but one person who had this secret, and he was
the legendary sage Utna-pishtim, an ancient king who was favored by the gods at the time the Deluge swept Mesopotamia,
who built a great boat into which he took his family, certain
craftsmen, and the animals to wait out the subsiding of the
waters. Utna-pishtim, whose name is taken to mean "He who
saw Life," is, of course, a kind of Noah, perhaps even the very
prototype of the Noah of the Book of Genesis. After the waters had abated, Utna-pishtim was taken to the "land of faraway Dilmun . . . in the garden of the sun." In a very old tablet
from Nippur, a Mesopotamian city as ancient as Uruk, it is
described how, when the world was very young and the work
of creation had just begun, Dilmun was a place "where the
croak of the raven was not heard, the bird of death did not
utter the cry of death, the lion did not devour, the wolf did
not rend the lamb, the dove did not mourn, there was no
widow, no sickness, no old age, no lamentation." Thus in the
paradisiacal land of Dilmun only Utna-pishtim and his wife
shared the great secret of eternal life. To the hoary sage-king
alone, of all living men, the gods had given immortality, for
he was the survivor of the Flood, with his family and with
"the seed of all living creatures," a true personification, we
suspect, of the biblical Noah.

Across the grasslands traveled Gilgamesh, searching for Dil-

mun, through mountain passes where no man ever trod, and
finally—by now almost a haunted man, wrapped in animal
skins, his face drawn, his cheeks sunken—he reached the garden of the gods at the edge of the sea (presumably at the Persian Gulf, either on the delta of the Tigris and Euphrates
rivers, or even somewhere on the Arabian coast). In the garden
by the water's edge Gilgamesh encountered a woman, Siduri,
the keeper of vineyards, the maker of wine.

Siduri thought Gilgamesh was nothing but a criminal who
was about to rape her, and so she bolted the gate against him.
But he convinced her that he was the famous Gilgamesh, king
of Uruk, who killed the Bull of Heaven and was now lament-
ing his brother Enkidu and, troubled by the knowledge that
death must come to him, was searching for eternal life.

Siduri asked:

> Why are you wandering like this?
> The life you seek you shall not find.
> When the gods created mankind
> They set death aside for man,
> Life they kept for themselves.
> O Gilgamesh, fill your belly,
> Have fun by day and by night,
> Make each day one of rejoicing,
> Day and night dance and play . . . .

But still Gilgamesh went on in his frantic search. He found
Utna-pishtim's boatman, Urshanabi. The king fated his journey by destroying the sacred talismanic stones Urshanabi kept
to protect his boat. But off they went, across the Sea of Death,
to Dilmun, to find Utna-pishtim.

Utna-pishtim was lying on his back, looking at the ap-
proaching boat.

There was some extended conversation between Gilgamesh and Utna-pishtim, in the manner of the East, in which important subjects are not immediately broached. At last Gilgamesh stated the question which was the object of his wanderings. "O father Utna-pishtim, you who have entered the assembly of the gods, how shall I find the life for which I am searching?"

But Utna-pishtim pushed his question aside and replied:

> Nothing is permanent.
> Do we build a house to stand forever?
> Do we sign contracts forever?
> Does the floodtime of rivers last?
> From the days of old there has been no permanence.
> The sleeping and the dead, how alike they are,
> Both like a painted death.
> Commoner and nobleman, what is different
> between them when they meet their fate?

Another enlightenment came to Gilgamesh, for he realized that Utna-pishtim and he were no different from each other in appearance. What is more, the sage was rather disappointing, for:

> I thought I should find you like a hero prepared
>   for battle,
> But you lie here taking your ease on your back.

To divert the wandering king Utna-pishtim told him the story of the Flood, how he took in all his gold, his animals, the craftsmen, how the rains fell. How after a while he sent out a swallow to see if the waters had abated; and the swallow returned. Then Utna-pishtim released a raven, who flew around, ate, cawed, but did not return. But the flood was not what Gilgamesh wanted to know about. He persisted with his questioning about the secret of immortality. At last the sage told him of a plant that brought eternal life, a plant lying at the bottom of a freshwater current in the ocean. Setting off with Utna-pishtim's boatman Urshanabi, Gilgamesh traveled on and on to the place where the plant was said to be, and dove into the waters to find it. He wanted to take it back to Uruk to give to the old men to eat. He wanted to call the plant "The Old Men are Young Again," he told the boatman, and he was going to eat it himself so that he could regain his lost youth. That night, while the two men, the king, and the boatman were sleeping, a serpent came from a well and ate the plant.

3

THE RIVERS

ANCIENT SUMER, THE SOUTHERN PORTION OF MESOPOTAMIA, IS a flat land with rich, black earth along its rivers and canals, dust and sand in the outlying deserts, and enigmatic ruins, mysterious and foreboding, in unexpected places. Clay shards—pieces of old pottery—litter the land, especially about the mounds, ignored by the Arabs grazing their flocks. The mounds are steep, eroded over the ages, covered with coarse vegetation. "Creations of Allah, the Almighty One," says the nomad sheep herder. The mounds are the remnants of cities, towns, and villages, layers and layers of them superimposed upon each other, slices of ancient civilizations and cultures one atop the other like a thick-tiered, Middle Eastern pastry of flaky dough, honey, cream, and nuts.

In the organized, modern Western world garbage is carted away on schedule and old buildings dismantled and put into an allotted hole in the ground. In the East and Middle East, where

much is built of clay brick, baked or raw, and the past garbage has been virtually all organic (only now is it iron, steel,
tin, rubber, and unregenerate plastic), the cities accumulated
their layers over the centuries. When a building, house, hovel,
palace, or temple collapsed from àge or the rains, the mud
bricks were not removed. The new edifice was built on the
remnants of the older one, and so on, until some mounds rose
seventy or eighty—even a hundred—feet above the plain.
These mounds are called *tells*, after the Arabic *tall*, meaning
mound. This economical system of not removing the wreckage
of previous buildings has been an unestimable aid to archaeologists, for thus they can trace a city's history through successive
stages, right down to bare earth.

Tells are found primarily in a great arc known as the Fertile
Crescent (though one might encounter them anywhere). The
Fertile Crescent is a long grid of rivers and waterways that
runs from the marshy, reedy delta that forms the mouth of the
joined Tigris and Euphrates rivers, where they enter the Persian Gulf, northward and westward across Syria to Turkey,
and then southward along the Mediterranean belt lands of
southern Turkey, coastal Syria, Lebanon, and Israel. A few
geographers continue the definition of the Fertile Crescent
into Egypt, where the Nile enters the Mediterranean. The
heartland of the Crescent is formed by the Tigris and the
Euphrates and their tributaries and the man-made canals that
cover the countryside. The western arm of the Crescent is, of
course, formed by other, lesser streams.

Mesopotamia has been much harried by its rivers. In Mesopotamian literature disasters, even invasions, are often expressed by the image of a flood. For the Sumerians and their
successors the Great Deluge is the watershed of history. Civilization, a kind of golden age such as man invariably fantasizes

the past, came to an end with the Flood, and both it and the
line of kings had to be renewed. And when the deluges were
not watery, they were composed of savage invaders. Like an
engulfing flood the Akkadians overran Uruk almost as brutally
as the deluvian waters had done half a century earlier. And
when the uncounted tribes of Semitic nomads burst upon
Sumer, they appeared as an onrushing flood of outland mi-
grants, inundating the land.

But no matter who rules, the riverways follow their own
paths through the Fertile Crescent, across the great undulating
plain, hemmed on three sides by mountain ranges and low-
lying hills, and on the fourth by the Arabian desert and the
waters of the Persian Gulf. To Mesopotamia's east are highlands, the Zagros Mountains of Persia, and north of them the
low, craggy mountains of Kurdistan. North are the mountains
of Armenia and the Taurus range of Turkey. On the west,
going south, are the mountains of Lebanon, through which
numerous passes lead to and from the Mediterranean. To the
southwest the Mesopotamian plain, hardly more than a desert
here, imperceptibly blends into the Arabian desert, that even
harsher land of rock-hard, asphaltlike surfaces and shifting
sands. The desert is relieved only by small oases and a few
cities (Mecca and Medina are the most famous) and the many
pocket-size kingdoms of the Arab potentates. The eastern
shores of the peninsula, like the rest of the Middle East, are a
vast graveyard of long-gone cities and towns, many lost in the
flowing sands and shifting coastline. On today's maps we can
see not only Kuwait but Abu Dhabi, Bahrein, and the Trucial
States' Muscat and Oman—"oil rich," as the current cliché
goes. In the past they were trading posts of great wealth. In
fact Bahrein, which has been specifically identified with the
legendary Dilmun (or Tilmun), where Gilgamesh visited

Utna-pishtim, the "faraway place" where death did not occur, was in later times a midway point for trade between India and the Mesopotamian cities, and perhaps even the Red Sea coast of Egypt.

But it is the rivers that concern us. Both the Euphrates and the Tigris begin not far from each other, near Lake Van, in the heart of Armenia (now split between Turkey, Iran and Russia). The Tigris, which starts within a bend of the Euphrates, heads due south, as if in a race to get to the joint meeting place, Karmat Ali, its dark, marshy waters hiding the secrets of a thousand towns and cities it has passed and even destroyed.

The Euphrates, some 2,100 miles in length (the Tigris is a few hundred miles shorter), heads almost due west, as if it were seeking an outlet in the Mediterranean, twisting and tumbling through deep gorges in Turkey's Taurus Mountains. Arrow-swift it runs, as if from the bow of some angry Assyrian warrior, through chrome-streaked, narrow canyons. When the sun strikes these ancient eroded walls, they shine like gold and porphyry, elements the ancients loved. The gorges widen, becoming liver-colored; tributaries join the rushing river. Soon the gorges are cut through open highlands covered with grass and stubble, with distant poplars offering a welcome relief from the harsh lands above, the lava masses from the Karacali volcano. In its first 110 miles the Euphrates drops 1,000 feet, or almost ten feet per mile, through rapids and cataracts.

The second phase of the Euphrates's run takes it through the Syrian plateau. By now it has turned a full ninety degrees and more to head toward the Persian Gulf, still across the Syrian-Iraqi plain. As it leaves Turkey, in the area the Greeks and Romans called Cappadocia, the river contributes greatly to the fertility of this otherwise barren land. The Roman geographer

Strabo noted that "the whole of this region is planted with fruit trees, the only country in all Cappadocia of which this is true, so that it produces not only the olive but also the monarite vine, which rivals the Greek vines." This second phase, across northern Syria, is the site of a number of old Greek and Roman kingdoms, settled by the Greco-Roman conquerors in small principalities to control the turbulent tribes of the region. They were poor kingdoms, the richest producing nothing better than gall nuts and medicinal plants, cattle, and slaves, all for export. It is a region marked by high, rocky soil, a bitter climate, wild asses, small fertile patches, and a simple and frugal prosperity. The Romans, in the first and second centuries A.D., complained on several occasions that the kings "had slaves but no coin"; one king, when pressed for a levy of troops for the Romans, replied that most of his male subjects had already been taken by the upper classes as slaves. The kings and nobility attended schools in Athens. They married Greek women, but the local influences were heavily Persian; along the upper Euphrates the people wore the loose trousers and sleeved tunics of the Persians.

On the upper plain the Euphrates is considerably slowed as it descends from about 650 feet above sea level to some 220 feet, dropping a mere seven inches a mile. Now it is less rigidly confined but still within definite channels, running through steep-sided valleys several hundred feet below the top of the plain. The walls of the valleys are formed of strata of marls and gypsum, underlying sandstone topped by a thin layer of desert breccia, a broken conglomerate rock of sharp edges and angular fragments that tear the feet of both beasts and men and reflect the heat and light. Here and there steps have been cut into the valley walls so that the women can descend to the river for water.

 Water is a precious commodity in the Middle East, and the great civilizations have always been founded along waterways. Now, with the aid of various United Nations agencies, irrigation of previously barren lands is being accomplished by deep-dug wells.

The second phase, the middle run of the river, is marked by the joining of several rivers of minor importance: the Sajur, Belikh, and Khabur, names unknown except outside their own lands. These are the larger tributaries in the area; others are not worth listing. Then there are a few dried beds of ancient streams that once flowed into the Euphrates and are now mere depressions on the desert floor.

The population in this area is sparse. There are few towns of any size, though they do spring up if they can receive enough water from the river by irrigation canals or from the huge waterwheels called *naurahs*. These wheels are often forty feet in diameter, and by means of jars and paddles they lift appreciable amounts of water into aqueducts. Mostly it is the small farmer who benefits from such simple but demanding systems, and development of the area stays at a minimum, for the energy and time required to bring water to the crops has prevented the growth of a high culture.

This economic and cultural backwater led the present Syrian government to build a gigantic barrage, or dam, at an obscure town called Medinat al Thawra, ninety miles east of Aleppo, the biggest city in the north of the country. The dam, 180 feet high and 4,500 feet wide, took seven years to build and cost three hundred million dollars (one hundred and forty million of which was lent by the Soviet government). Completed in 1975, it turned out to be a formidable project, employing 10,000 Syrian laborers (mainly villagers) and 5,000 Russian technicians. Eight turbines were installed, to furnish 400,000 kilowatts of power, and the waters are expected to irrigate one and a half million acres sometime in the future. Even as the barrage was being completed, the entire economy of Syria had been changed for the better. Medinat al Thawra grew to become a bustling city of seventy thousand people, due largely to the influx of workers and their families. But new roads had to be built to carry the traffic from suddenly burgeoning farms and industries. Wheat and cotton, poultry and cattle farms, even flowers, became mainstays of the new agriculture; hundreds of large and small factories, fertilizer plants, refineries for petroleum by-products (Syria is an oil producer), and plastics factories draw their power from the new turbines.

But downstream, in Iraq, which did not share in the new Syrian bounty, farms began to dry up because the waters of the Euphrates were being stored in a huge reservoir, a man-made lake of sparkling blue-green named after the Syrian president, General Assad. Iraq claimed that not only was it being prevented from getting its accustomed share of the river's waters and not benefiting from the annual floods, which are an age-old method of irrigating the adjoining farmlands, but also the dangerously low level was producing swamps that attracted mosquitoes. The health of the people was being threatened. Both countries moved troops about, more as shows of force than as an actual step to war. Intervention by leaders of other Arab nations brought a promise by Syria to allow more water to flow into Iraq, but even so, downstream the tiny plots of eggplants and tomatoes and pepper plants were wilting and the waterwheels were barely scooping up anything to irrigate the crops.

Though the barrage has been a great help to the farms of this part of the Syrian plain, the areas close to the banks of the Euphrates have always enjoyed a reputation for fertility. Here, unlike the princes of Cappadocia, the Roman-backed kings were richer—opulent is an apt description—with many jewels and much gold, made wealthy not by war, the traditional means to quick riches (or to immediate poverty), but by the regular flow of trade through the infinitesimal kingdoms. Whoever controlled the trade routes controlled the sources of income, for a kingdom was delineated by whatever roads and cultivated areas a king could defend.

Even before the barrage the land was one of impressive fertility and beauty: garden patches, small hamlets, pistachio trees, groves of olives. Although beautiful in its simplicity, the barrage also has been a welcome change.

The river soon widens its banks. It is now in Iraq, having crossed the border at a town called Hit. It has here the dreadful tendency to wander without reason, and like other rivers with undefined banks upon which towns and cities have been founded, it shows a dismaying love of changing course without warning, leaving once-important centers isolated and bereft of meaning and communication. In the seven hundred miles through lower Mesopotamia, before it merges with the Tigris, its rate of flow is barely perceptible, dropping less than four inches per mile, and in the last one hundred miles only an inch per mile. But along this stretch have been founded some of the greatest cities of antiquity, among them Babylon, Uruk, and Ur, while nearby, on adjoining waterways, have been Kish, Nippur, and Eridu, as well as the very ancient, seminal site of al-Ubaid, the earliest of the Sumerian cities and the one which has given its name as an alternative to "Sumerian," a definitive term for the first great civilization.

Somewhere in here was once Eden, with its garden in which God placed Adam before the creation of Eve, and where Eve was taken from Adam's rib.

And the Lord God planted a garden eastward in Eden; and there he put the man whom he had formed. And out of the ground made the Lord God to grow every tree that is pleasant to the sight, and good for food; the tree of life also in the midst of the garden, and the tree of the knowledge of good and evil.

"Eden" is derived from the Sumerian word for steppe— *an–edena*—which refers specifically to a lush, elevated area between the cities of Uruk, Larsa, Badtibira, and Zabalam. Lagash, a city on the Euphrates north of Uruk, had a running battle with another neighbor, Umma, over their use of the common watercourse and the possession of certain steppe and grazing lands, called *Gu-edena*, the "edge of Eden." The war, which started before the twenty-sixth century B.C., went on for generations, until Umma sacked Lagash and looted its temples. But this defeat for Lagash did not end the quarreling and bitterness, which lasted until both cities were overrun by the new power of Agade about the twenty-fourth century B.C.

The Tigris, the more easterly of the twin rivers, is also the straighter. Descending in a torrent from the Taurus range, it enters the Mesopotamian desert sooner, and on its higher stretches offers better conditions for civilization. In upper Iraq it flows through a gentle triangle of fertile land between hills and desert, upon which the ancient city of Nineveh was founded. Today's Mosul, a great oil center, lies across the Tigris from Nineveh, which is now nothing but a mass of sand-covered tells under excavation. Farther down are two great barrages erected in ancient times, of such excellent workmanship that huge fragments still block the river from upstream navigation. A pair of rivers, the Greater Zab and the Lesser Zab, flowing down from Kurdistan on the east, join the Tigris below Nineveh and Mosul. Between these two rivers, which are about sixty miles apart, lie the ruins of the famed and notorious Asshur, the capital of the Assyrians. The town that adjoins the ruins is called Kalaat Sharqat and is an important railhead. Continuing south the plain is marked everywhere by traces of ancient irrigation systems, but today few people

The sandy deserts of the Arabian peninsula adjoining Mesopotamia have been notoriously bereft of water. Today
sheikdoms such as Kuwait, drawing water from the Gulf
of Arabia and desalinating it, are developing vast hydroponic
"gardens."

work the land. Finally the Tigris reaches Samarra, or Sumere, once an important center and for a while a capital for both Arabs and Persians. In the past the river in this area was partially controlled by a canal system, but today it is unconfined and allowed to follow its own whims. Below Samarra there are ruins of innumerable ancient cities and towns, and of the great metropolis of Baghdad, one of the most fabled cities of the world. Today's Baghdad is not the ancient one, but a series of old suburbs grown into a single unit. Here the Tigris and Euphrates are only about thirty-five miles apart; they were even closer in the past and were tied together by irrigation canals. Next come old—but not ancient—ruins, those of the cities of Ctesiphon, on the left bank, and Seleucia on the right; both date from the Greco-Roman period. The river has wandered badly at this point, and no ancient ruins can be found along its banks; some small cities and towns are all it can boast of.

Shortly the Tigris joins the Euphrates to form the Shatt-al-Arab. Now both waters have entered a vast, marshy, reedy, swampy delta of black silt carried from as far away as Armenia and everywhere in between. Blinding sun, withering heat, marsh Arabs living—anthropologists and archaeologists suppose—fairly much as the earliest of the Sumerians did, in tiny settlements of wattled houses, getting about on reed boats. As the sweet waters of the Shatt-al-Arab blend into the salt waters of the Persian Gulf, it is hard to distinguish wetlands from the sea, glistening and blinding in the sun. But there is a major channel here, leading from Basra, an inland port of the Euphrates, to all the oceans of the world. From here the Mesopotamians could reach out to Egypt, Africa, India, and beyond, transporting both material goods and the ideas that were so fertile in the great arc of the Crescent.

4

THE NEOLITHIC REVOLUTION

THE FIRST GRAIN, IN SUMERIAN TRADITION, WAS BROUGHT DOWN by An, the sky god, who gave the people wheat, barley, and hemp. But Enlil, the god of royal power, took it away, storing it in a pile in the hill country, "barring the mountains as with a door." But then the gods Nanzu and Ninmada "allowed Sumer, the land that knows no grain, to come to know grain."

This is a mythological manner of saying that the first agriculture was developed in the highlands and mountains around the great plain of the Fertile Crescent. Ringing the area are the uplands of Afghanistan, Iran, northern Iraq, southern and eastern Turkey, and the western ranges that form barriers to the Mediterranean. Here conditions were favorable for the growth of food grains, while they were not on the plain. In 1967, while investigating the probable and possible sources of basic foods, the American agronomist J. R. Harlan conducted an interesting experiment. He made a sickle frame of wood, with sharp pieces of flint as the cutting edge, basing the design on similar implements discovered at Neolithic sites in the Middle East. Imagining that he was a member of a late Stone Age family, Harlan harvested in an hour a kilogram (2.2 pounds) of ripe, wild wheat. He knew that the wheat, when full-grown, had a mature period of about three weeks before the ears (as the seed pods are called) fell to the ground. Harlan estimated that in this short period a Stone Age family could have harvested enough wild wheat to last until the following year's wild wheat had grown and was ready for gathering. Without working very hard the family could have cut a ton of grain.

Clearly such a family, with some hunting and fishing and gathering of other wild foods—berries, roots, and nuts among them—could have lived very well, without the trouble of planting, watering, and weeding a field of grain. Harlan and his colleague, Daniel Zohary, had found that the wild ancestors of our present-day wheats grew here in profusion. They reported that "over many thousands of hectares [a hectare is 2.471 acres] it would be possible to harvest wild wheat today from natural stands almost as dense as a cultivated wheat field."

> Domestication may not have taken place where the wild cereals were most abundant. Why should anyone cultivate a cereal where natural stands are almost as dense as a cultivated field? . . . Farming itself may have originated in areas adjacent to, rather than in, the regions of greatest abundance of wild cereals.

But somewhere mankind changed both diet and ways of living by developing domesticated grains. It was a change of tremendous consequences. The historian V. Gordon Childe, writing early in this century, called the transformation from a simple hunting and gathering economy into an agricultural economy "the Neolithic Revolution," but it was a revolution that did not happen overnight nor in a few weeks nor over a century (as did that other, later great change, the Industrial Revolution), but over tens of centuries, over millennia.

Excavations at a vast number of Neolithic sites, primitive settlements, and even some early villages and towns, among them Jericho, Çatal Haycuk, and Jarmo, all on the highlands that fringe the Fertile Crescent, have produced numerous clues to the development of agriculture, which in turn made the growth of civilization possible. Childe had thought that a change in climate, the ending of the Ice Age, had made it possible for towns and cities to evolve. But in the eyes of latter-day archaeologists and anthropologists, aided by scientists in other fields, the changes were due to other factors. The reasons for the Neolithic Revolution are complicated, and I can give only a few of the most important ones here. The two primary reasons are the development of edible grains and useful plants and the domestication of certain animals. Some scholars have pointed out that Neolithic man did not necessarily need to develop intensive agriculture: The reasons that he did may never be known. Hunting-gathering societies are not necessarily impoverished. Many had and may have (there are a few remaining survivors) not only more than adequate high-quality nourishment, and good and warm shelter, but a complex and interesting social life, with music, dancing, art, and literature (the latter being oral rather than written). About the latter the British archaeologist Sir Mortimer Wheeler aspishly comments:

There is perhaps a tendency on the part of the modern mind to overestimate the value of literacy; certain it is that

the unscribbled brain is capable of remarkable feats of re-
tention and calculation.

There must have been sure and certain reasons—pressures, or
the need for variety, or temporary or recurring famines, or
even curiosity—that led to the involved steps that brought
about the development of wild grains into domesticated ones.

Hans Helbaek, a Danish palaeoethnobotanist (that is, someone who works with the plant life of prehistoric times), by
years-long analysis of the grains, spikelets, husks, and stems of
plants found by archaeologists, which he compared with the
corresponding parts of contemporary plants, found that the
first three crop plants domesticated by man in the Middle East
were two types of wheat and one of barley. The wheats were
einkorn, scientifically called *Triticum monococcum*, and
emmer, *Triticum dicoccum*. The barley was *Hordeum vulgare*.

The cultivated forms of einkorn wheat, Helbaek and others
have found, probably descended from a wild variety of einkorn, *Triticum boeoticum*. Both have similar chromosome
structures and can be crossbred. Wild einkorn has been found
in southern Turkey, northern Syria, and northern Iraq, fringe
lands of the Fertile Crescent.

In the same manner cultivated emmer wheat can be assumed
to have come from wild emmer wheat, *Triticum diccoides*.
Again both plants have similar chromosome structures. From
the hybrid a durum, or hard, wheat (*Triticum durum*) developed. They are known as "naked" wheats, highly evolved and
hence easier for Neolithic people to husk and grind into flour.
Wild emmer wheat is found in the western highlands of the
Fertile Crescent.

But these wheats, serviceable as they might have been, are
not our modern bread wheats, which came from a more com-

plex breeding process. Bread wheat—*Triticum aestivum*—is not found in wild form, and it appeared on the prehistoric scene one-to-two thousand years after the first use of emmer and einkorn. A giant leap forward was needed to produce this younger and more palatable form of wheat. The emmer-durum lines of wheat were hybridized with a plant known as goat-face grass, *Aegilops squarrosa*. Goat-face grass has a genetic structure compatible to the emmer wheats, and modern wheat is a combination—a totality—of the two chromosome complexes. But this hybridization was not something that happened offhandedly. The two grasses do not grow in the same area, for, as we have seen, wild emmer wheat grows on the western fringes of the Fertile Crescent, but goat-face grass in its original wild state grew on the easternmost sections of the Fertile Crescent and well up into the mountain ranges that form Afghanistan and northwestern India, being a hardy plant that withstands cold climates.

These two plants, geographically and one might say "psychologically" separated, had to be brought together. Even if they grew next to each other in the wild state, the crossbreed is an unwanted plant, being weak and dwarfed. Somehow wandering tribes planted cultivated emmer wheat in areas where goat-face grass thrived, and the two crossbred. Whether one person or many noticed that this brought an entirely new plant, of unusual and better qualities, we can never know, nor are we likely to learn if the hybrid came about by chance or by deliberate experimentation, and over how long a period. But eventually, by a process of watching, selection, breeding, and experimenting, over and over again, an entirely new form of wheat developed.

Barley, which has a similar structure, was also bred out of a primitive wild form into a domesticated form. Later other plants, particularly flax, which produces the fiber from which linen is made and also a valuable oil, and cotton, one of the most important of all plants, underwent processes of domestication. Beans, squashes, cabbages, and onions were also domesticated early, along with the selective cultivation of fruit-bearing trees, including the apple, olive, fig, orange, and date. With the pressing of olives and grapes and the fermentation of grain for beer, fired pottery containers become indispensable. As in the case of bread wheat, many other plants do not exist in a nondomesticated state. Some of the developments in selectivity and hybridization go so far back that such examples as the opium poppy, the first of the pain-killers, are no longer found wild.

What is worth emphasizing is that while cultivated plants—wild plants sown deliberately by people—can revert to the wild and thrive, domesticated plants—those deliberately developed for the use of mankind—need people for survival, for sowing, watering, weeding, and harvesting in an endless repetition of the cycle, otherwise they die out.

I have perhaps reduced the complexities of Neolithic botany to too few essentials. The American botanist Oakes Ames adds a further note that fleshes out this sparse picture:

> The most important annuals are unknown in their wild state. They first appear in association with man. They are as much a part of his history as the worship of the gods to whose beneficence he attributed the origin of wheat and barley. Therefore, their appearance simultaneously on the historic scene indicates a greater age for agriculture than the archaeologists and anthropologists have allowed.

Cultivation of gardens and fields brought about a change in living habits. People could now remain in one place instead of wandering about according to the migratory habits of animals, or the availability of stands of wild wheat and barley and rye.

Somewhere in this period came the invention of bread, from grains ground more or less fine and baked on a flat, hot stone, either atop a fire or at its edge, or perhaps even in the dying ashes. From a study of archaeological evidence we know how bread was made. We cannot know the exact details of baking, however (which in any case would vary from one area to another). Even today different yet similar breads are made, among them the flat, crisp breads called *lavash* by the Armenians, and the whole-wheat, flat bread called *naan* by the Kurds. In contemporary terms the recipe for Neolithic bread is:

> 2 cups of either sifted whole wheat or unbleached
>   white flour
> ⅔ cup of water
> pinch of salt
> sesame seeds

Mix the flour, salt, and water together in a container (an earthenware bowl if one wants to be "authentic"). A slight bit more of water or of flour may be needed: The Neolithic baker—usually a woman—probably measured by eye and by the feel of the dough. Knead for about five minutes on a floured board. Break the dough into two portions and set them aside, covered, for about half an hour.

If you are using a charcoal fire, let it burn down to hot coals, with the flat stone atop them; a modern baker turns the oven to its highest. The next step is to roll out each ball of dough as flat as possible, into a round of about fourteen inches. (I have seen West Asian women flatten whole-wheat dough by hand, stretching and patting it into the proper shape.) The

 The discovery of methods by which wild wheat could be hybridized into a palatable form is one of the great culinary and gastronomic advances of mankind. The village baker, turning out loaves of delicious, fragrant flat bread is still common in the Middle East. Villagers who have no ovens of their own (they cook on small charcoal fires) bring their great casserole pots to the baker for cooking.

dough may resist at first, but it can be rolled very thin and flat. Wet the top of the flattened loaf with water, sprinkle with sesame seeds, and gently roll the seeds into the dough. The oven or fire should now be at its hottest. Fold the loaf loosely over a long stick or rod (one can even use a yard stick) and place it on a baking tin on the floor of the oven and unroll it. Cook for two to three minutes. The surface will have bubbled. The bread will now be baked; it should be lightly browned. It can be placed under the oven grill for twenty to thirty seconds to brown the top.

Such was the basic method of baking bread all over the Middle East, from Egypt to Persia and beyond. Many Indian peasants use a similar method to produce a flat, whole-wheat loaf called the *chapati*, which they bake for about a minute on a flat metal pan over a hot fire. Yeast bread appeared eventually. Yeast is a natural component of air and the soil, and it was an inevitable event for yeast to "contaminate" dough set aside for later baking. The dough rose in the heat of the fire and produced a better, or at least different, more palatable loaf. Under the watchful eye of Neolithic woman and man the dough became responsive to the human touch; part of the risen dough would be set aside to leaven the next batch, and so on. Yeast bread led to another interesting product, beer, a radical addition to the diet of ancient peoples. Yeast was directly connected with the baking of breads, and early bakers were also brewers. At some point in the Neolithic Revolution it was discovered that germinated seeds made a better, more palatable flour, the seeds, after germination, being dried and ground.

Again we cannot know the exact moment when beer was discovered—it may have been one of those fortuitous discoveries made a number of times in different places—but it was clearly the result of putting together a number of observations of natural phenomena. Barley was the key ingredient—germinated, dried, and ground. At this stage it would have been ready for bread-making, but somehow a batch of barley in a bowl must have received several times its bulk in water, perhaps during a rain storm. The resulting liquid fermented from yeast spores in the air, and then there was beer. Once the principle was known, it was a simple process to make beer with a lump of uncooked leavened bread dough as the fermenting agent. The Greeks (this was two or three thousand years after the discovery of fermented grain products) complained that the Mesopotamians were addicted to beer, which is why their own god Dionysus, the deity of wine and revelry, fled the land. It has been estimated that 40 percent of the Sumerians' grain went into beer. A temple workman received a liter (somewhat over a quart) of beer a day, and higher officials as much as five liters. There were eight kinds of barley beer, eight of wheat, and three mixed. The varieties probably came from the addition of flavorings such as spices and herbs, a practice the Egyptians are known to have used.

Two other plants of value in the Neolithic Revolution might be mentioned, both of great esteem in the eyes of the ancient peoples. They are the flax and cotton plants. Flax is the plant that produces the raw material for linen. It is an annual and has strong, tough fibers in its stem which are separated from the softer tissues by a process called "retting." These fibers were and are woven into threads which produce a fabric of great versatility. The flax seeds produce an edible oil—linseed oil—of many uses, and the residual oil cake that results after pressing is used as food for cattle.

Cotton is a plant of even greater versatility. It is a small shrub bearing large pods, or bolls. These "flowers," which con-

tain seeds surrounded by long white fibers, run in length from
¾ to 2½ inches. The fibers can be spun into a thread from
which cloth of varying degrees of fineness and quality can be
made. This cloth is strong, durable, and easy to launder. Cotton clothing made it possible for the mountain and hill peoples to shed their heavy furs and woolens and move down into
the steamy river valleys, not only of Mesopotamia but China,
India, and Egypt. Cotton is an extremely satisfactory apparel
for the hot and humid tropics, for going naked or seminaked
is often impossible in the burning sun; one must be clothed at
least partially to protect the skin and avoid sunstroke. Cotton,
like flax, produces an oil of much value, and again the residue
of the crushed seed cake is fed to cattle.

With the development of agriculture and the abandonment
of hunting as a major source of food, new forms of society developed. Hunting bands were usually small and democratic,
with a chief who might be supreme during the hunt but whose
authority lessened at the encampment after enough game had
been killed for food. With the spread of agriculture as the
major basis for food, new demands were made upon the group.
Farming meant land in quantity, and this involved control of
land. In the beginning land was held in common by the tribe,
clan, or extended family. As towns developed land was, in
most cases, held communally by the entire town. From indica-
tions in the earliest of the surviving literature, and from par-
allels in some small contemporary societies, town leaders were
elected on a democratic basis by councils, which might be
composed of the elders or a special group, or by the entire
adult community. But the power of these leaders was limited;
a leader like Gilgamesh would have supreme power in times of
emergency or need: war, famine or flood, the building of a
new temple, the celebration of some special religious event.

In later days Gilgamesh, though possessing tremendous powers and considered a king, was still subject to the will of a two-part, or bicameral, council of elders and of the entire adult community. When Agga, king of Kish, the most important of the Sumerian cities and one of the original from the predeluvian ages, demanded tribute of Uruk, Gilgamesh had to ask permission of the city elders to fight instead. But the elders preferred to submit and enjoy peace. Gilgamesh then called an assembly of the men of Uruk, who decided to fight rather than submit. Pleased with the support he had gained, Gilgamesh went to war against Agga, who had suddenly appeared before the walls of Uruk. The Sumerian poem which recounts the event is vague about the outcome; apparently Gilgamesh came to terms with Agga without a war. But the point of this anecdote is that the Sumerian cities were in a transition between the rough democracy of the old hunting societies and the beginning of a new societal form in which the kings were all-powerful. When they reached the point of being considered divine, or semidivine as well, then ownership of everything passed to them. Ostensibly the king held the land on behalf of the city's titular deity, but in fact, it was he who had absolute power, over the land and all that it produced, and over the farmers who produced the wealth that grew upon the land. For with the growth of agriculture the men and women of the hunting-gathering societies had changed their status from that of free people to that of serfs and slaves. And this is the way it was to be for many centuries afterward.

The domestication of animals is a question which has not yet been satisfactorily answered. In fact questions multiply without a chance of clarification. Why were the goat and sheep selected for domestication and not the antelope? How were

 On a barren hillside overlooking the vast Mesopotamian plain a farmer prepares for spring planting. His equipment is simple: a wooden plough drawn by oxen, hardly different from that used millenia ago. The domestication of animals, among them the ox, and the discovery of regular planting and of hybridizing of wild grasses, enabled early man to settle down in village societies.

the pig and cow domesticated? Most informed guesses put the dog and the pig early, if not first, on the list of animals to be taken into the household. They were probably the two animals that stayed around villages, for both, in the wild state, are scavengers, curious and adventurous, and the supposition is that they both rooted around in early garbage piles and became accustomed to people and were soon tamed. Such domestication came around 8000 B.C., if not earlier. The oldest domesticated bones of all, of goats, have been found in a site in the Zagros Mountains in west central Iran. Dates for dogs, pigs, and goats and other domesticated animals are set for a thousand years later at Jarmo, in Iraq, and Çatal Huyuk, in southern Turkey.

I must mention one more major transformation in ancient life before we descend again to the Mesopotamian plains. The roles of man and woman changed. Man was the hunter, woman the gatherer. Despite some theories that man was born a natural warrior and permanently aggressive, it seems likely that man did not practice war until social conditions brought about enough crowding so that war became an economic necessity as much as an outlet for overwhelming machismo. As people became settled, the role of woman took on new dimensions. Lewis Mumford has given us a good précis of woman's role at this period.

> Many scholars who have no difficulty in recognizing that tools are mechanical counterfeits of the muscles and limbs of the male body—that the hammer is a fist, the spear a lengthened arm, the pincers the human fingers—seem prudishly inhibited against the notion that woman's body is also capable of extrapolation. They recoil from the notion that the womb is a primitive container and the breast a pitcher of milk: For that reason they fail to give full significance to the appearance of a large variety of containers precisely at

the moment when we know from other evidence that woman was beginning to play a more distinctive role as food-provider and effective ruler than she had in the earlier foraging and hunting economies. The tool and the utensil, like the sexes themselves, perform complementary functions. One moves, manipulates, assaults, the other remains in place, to hold and protect and preserve. . . .

Cooking, milking, dyeing, tanning, brewing, gardening are, historically, female occupations: All derive from handling the vital processes of fertilization, growth, and decay, or the life-arresting processes of sterilization and preservation. All these functions necessarily enlarge the role of containers: indeed are inconceivable without baskets, pots, bins, vats, barns; while true domesticity, with its intimate combination of sexuality and responsible parenthood, comes in only with the permanent dwelling house, the cattlefold, and the settled village.

The creation of moisture-proof, leak-proof, vermin-proof clay vessels to store grain, oil, wine, and beer was essential to the entire Neolithic economy and gave it stability and the basis upon which to grow imaginatively.

THE SUMERIANS

TWO CENTURIES AGO, WHEN WESTERN SCHOLARS BEGAN TO search out the Middle East for ancient cities, the existence of Sumer was not even suspected. What the scholars—many of whom were but gifted amateurs—wanted to know about were the peoples of the Bible, especially the Assyrians, Babylonians, and Persians, all of whom were known to the classical Greeks. Assyria and Babylon seemed to be not only keys to ancient knowledge, but keys to ancient civilization itself. Now they have taken second place to the Sumerians, from whom much of ancient and even modern civilization stems.

The Sumerians were a highly cultured people, first appearing about 4500 B.C., at a place now called al-Ubaid (hence Sumerian culture is sometimes called "Ubaid"). The people at al-Ubaid and the other cities did not call themselves Sumerians; that name was applied later by the Akkadians, who conquered them. They lived primarily on the southern half of the Mesopotamian river system. The upper half, which later saw urban civilization, was called Assyria, and when Babylon rose to unite both sections, the entire area, north and south, came to be known as Babylonia. The Sumerians were a fairly homogenized people, much alike physically, as studies of skeletal remains show. Skeletons from the late level of Eridu, one of the southernmost cities close to al-Ubaid, where the dead were buried stretched out on their backs in rectangular brick tombs, show a surprisingly large body size. This would be from a period about 3500 B.C. or earlier. Graves a thousand years later show people of a smaller frame. This decline may be due either to the result of some other, unidentified race intermingling with the Sumerians, or perhaps—more likely—it was caused by the trend, noted by anthropologists, of succeeding generations of early people to decline in size as they changed from hunting to agriculture, the hunters having both a better diet and better health.

The origin of the Sumerians is still open to question. There are two major theories, and it is always possible that they stem from a combination of both. One theory is that they came from Susa, the central city of Elam, a land on the western slopes of the Zagros Mountains and the central Iranian plateau. Before that one can only surmise that they had wandered down from the vast Asian steppes, homeland of so many peoples. The second theory is that they came from the sea. There is a Sumerian tradition reported by Greek historians that a fisherman swam up the Persian Gulf bringing with him the gifts of civilization. The Greek name of the fisherman was Oannes. He could be Enki, the Sumerian god of the waters, who was also the tutelary god of Eridu, which lies on a lagoon on the Persian Gulf and is known as the first of the five cities that existed before the Flood. Beyond Eridu, out in the Gulf, is the legendary Dilmun, the mystical home of the Sumerians and possibly older than Eridu.

Granting the possibility of an arrival by sea, how then did the Sumerians take to the ocean, and from where? Again we have to deal with speculation. There is some kind of connection between Sumer and the cities of the Indus Valley, in western India (now Pakistan). From the evidence of certain artifacts in the Indus Valley the story of Gilgamesh and Enkidu was known. And Enki looks suspiciously like the Indian deity Narayana. Enki in Sumerian art is portrayed by streams of water flowing from his shoulders, streams in which fish are shown swimming upstream. Narayana is a fish god and is identified with the great Lord Vishnu, whose first appearance on earth was as a fish (his second and third incarnations were as a tortoise and a boar, respectively). The Indian scholar D. D. Kosambi states authoritatively that the name Narayana is not Indian but Mesopotamian, and "seems to be 'he who sleeps upon the flowing waters' . . . and this is taken as the steady state of Narayana. It precisely describes the Mesopotamian Ea, and Enki, who sleeps in his chambers in the midst of the waters, as Sumerian myth and many a Sumerian seal tell us." One more connection might be noted: The Sumerians described themselves as "black-headed," and it is known that the early Indus people were called "black" by their enemies. But neither race was Negroid, merely dark-skinned. Still none of this proves either the origin of the Sumerians or an affinity to the people of the Indus Valley, and we must await still more discoveries to give us a better answer.

What we do know shows the Sumerians to have been a tremendously gifted and imaginative people. Their language, as deciphered from clay tablets, was an interesting and complex one, and one which has no relationship to any other language, either ancient, medieval, or modern. It exists in solitary splendor, telling us about heroes and kings, businessmen, teachers, schoolboys, warriors, medicines, inventories, gardening, and almost every activity and role known in the past. We can credit the Sumerians with the very important discovery of the art of writing (if other people had it before them, that fact is for the present still unknown), for with it a simple village life could develop into an elaborate civilization. Writing, as the Sumerians practiced it, in virtually every phase of existence, demanded schools for an educated elite and for the many scribes who were needed for all the recordkeeping and letter writing they liked to do. Thus the Sumerians had the earliest known schools. Thousands of schoolboys' exercise tablets have been found, along with word lists and textbooks. Writing produced not only business records but the earliest known epic literature, obviously oral at first but written down in quite primitive times. Laws, pharmacopoeias, library catalogs, agricultural methods, love songs, moral ideas, folk stories, jokes, fables, laments, psalms, maps, and curses flowed from their styluses, as well as lists by the hundreds if not the thousands—lists of kings, words, imports, exports, inventories, books, or almost anything else the mind could imagine. They could write about moral concerns, psychological warfare, the theme of man's resurrection from the dead, floods and famines, and the means to alleviate the suffering these caused. They could write down laws to protect the weak and the widowed, the poor and the homeless; they could draw maps of their world and their cities; they could create animal fables to express human follies and weaknesses and their troubles with their children. One text complains of the problems a father has with his son. The father

A house in Ur, about the time of the biblical patriarch Abraham, roughly the eighteenth century B.C. *As is still practiced today, living arrangements centered around an open court; family and clan privacy was and is highly esteemed.*

asks his son, who apparently had been hanging around the town square, "Where were you?"

The answer is, "Nowhere."

"If you didn't go anywhere, where were you?" And so on. The father complains that he never made his son do manual labor—plowing the fields, digging, carrying cane—never made the son support him. The son, the father complains, wastes each day "in pleasures" and has become nothing but "fat, big, broad, powerful, and puffed."

The full extent of Sumerian civilization wasn't realized until the 1920s and 1930s, when the English archaeologist, Sir Leonard Woolley, excavated the city of Ur, one of the southernmost cities, near al-Ubaid and Eridu. Ur resembled other Sumerian cities in structure and function, being the center of a small state. Woolley thought that Ur went back far beyond the Flood into the dim period when the Euphrates Valley's lower end was still a great marsh through which the waters of the twin rivers made their sluggish way into the ocean. Gradually the marshland began to fill in and dry up as the rivers brought down more and more silt from the north. "Islands" of solid land, composed of rich alluvial soil, began to form in the marshes. One of these islands was the site for Ur.

Early man established small settlements on Ur and the other islands that appeared. Huts were constructed of mud and wattle or slight timber frames filled with reed mats, with floors of beaten mud and fireplaces of mud or crude brick, and wooden doors whose hinge poles turned on stone sockets. In such settlements fine-worked pottery has been found, along with rougher household wares used for cooking and storage, hoes and adzes of chipped and polished stone, saw-toothed flints and flakes of imported volcanic glass, and sickles made of hard-baked clay. The settlers were no longer hunters and

 Sir Leonard Woolley, at the right, dressed impeccably as if for a brisk walk in the English countryside, labors under the burning Mesopotamian sun clearing a grave at Ur. (Mrs. Woolley in her modish cloche hat and women's plus-fours has her back to her husband.) Sir Leonard had entered into a great rivalry with two other British archaeologists in a race to uncover the best and the most exotic treasures. In Egypt Howard Carter was finding and looting the fabulous tomb of King Tutankhamen, while in the Indus Valley John Marshall hoped—without luck—to find similar royal tombs to those of Ur and the Nile.

gatherers but agriculturists, cultivating the land and reaping harvests of grain; they kept domesticated cattle, sheep, and goats; they fished in the marshes, had looms for weaving, and wore ornaments of shell or crudely chipped, transparent white quartz, carnelian, and obsidian.

They were a primitive, if not barbarous, people on these island settlements. Woolley thinks they may have been one of the many Semitic-speaking peoples that inhabited the land as far west as the Mediterranean Sea and south into the Arabian peninsula. But they were not Sumerians. The Sumerians could not envisage a time when they did not have all the appurtenances of civilization, and they seem to have appeared at Ur and elsewhere already fully civilized, taking over the primitive settlements and immediately turning them into cities. They put up permanent buildings of burned brick and stout, outer defensive walls. The primitive people were not driven out but seemed to have been taken in as serfs or slaves. For later generations this is the way it always was. The Sumerian expert S. N. Kramer writes:

Bound by his particular world view, the Sumerian thinker saw historical events as coming ready-made and "full-grown, full-blown" on the world scene, and not as the slow product of man's interaction with his environment. He believed, for example, that his own country, Sumer, which he knew as a land of thriving cities and towns, villages and farms, in which flourished a well-developed assortment of political, religious, and economic institutions and techniques, had always been more or less the same from the very beginning of days— that is, from the moment the gods had planned and decreed it to be so, following the creation of the universe. That Sumer had once been desolate marshlands with but few scattered settlements, and had only gradually come to be

what it was after many generations of struggle and toil,
marked by human will and determination, man-laid plans
and experiment and diverse fortunate discoveries and in-
ventions—such thoughts probably never occurred to the
most learned of the Sumerian sages.

All of Ur and its sister cities is interesting, but at Ur there
was found something that rose above all else in drama and
importance. The discovery over a period of several years of a
series of royal tombs revealed something of both the social
structure of Sumer and its culture. Woolley found private
graves dating, in his estimate, as early as 3100 B.C., but the royal
graves, he believed, went back as far as 3500 B.C. and covered
a span of about three hundred years. Many of the tombs had
been robbed at various times; some of the thieves seemed to
have been Sumerian workmen who looted older tombs while
building new ones. The graves of even private citizens were
rather elaborate. The body was wrapped in a roll of matting
or placed in a coffin of wickerwork, wood or even clay. It
lay on its right side in a fetal position, with the hands before
the face, holding a cup which might have once been filled with
water, and accompanied in the grave by various utensils—
vessels of clay, copper or stone, and weapons and tools. The
coffin might contain jewelry, a knife or dagger, and perhaps
a cylinder seal, which was the equivalent of the owner's own
signature or mark. Woolley believes these preparations show
a concern for the welfare of an individual in the afterlife,
which was viewed as some kind of journey to faraway places,
or a descent into another world.

The royal tombs are far more elaborate. Some of them are
structures of as many as four rooms. The archaeologists were
disappointed at the large number of them that were plundered,

but in the winter of 1927–28 they stumbled upon a series of
tombs that were either intact or only partially robbed. In them
they found, first, the bodies of retainers, most of them women,
in groups of five, eight, or ten, and one group of sixty-eight.
"The sight of the remains of the victims is gruesome," remarked Woolley, for it was clear that these attendants, women
and men, had been members of the court and had been immo-
lated with the king or queen they served. Some of the finds are
worth noting. After unearthing five bodies in an ordinary
grave, Woolley says:

> We came to another group of bodies, those of ten women
> carefully arranged in two rows; they wore headdresses of
> gold, lapis lazuli, and carnelian, and elaborate bead necklaces.
> . . . At the end of the row lay the remains of a wonderful
> harp, the wood of its frame decayed but its decoration in-
> tact.

The harp was decorated with gold, a mosaic in red stone,
lapis lazuli, and white shell, and topped with the splendid head
of a bull wrought in gold with eyes and beard of lapis lazuli.
Across the ruins of the harp lay the bones of the gold-crowned
harpist. After that treasures were found in profusion: a
wooden sledge-chariot decorated in gold and jewels and mosaic, with the bodies of the asses that pulled it and the drivers
lying before it. Also among the finds were a gaming board;
tools and weapons, including a saw made of gold; stone and
copper bowls; masses of vessels in copper, silver, and stone; silver religious vessels; tall, slender, silver tumblers nested inside
each other; gold tumblers and a chalice; bowls of gold; lions'
heads in silver; and more bodies.

As Woolley progressed through the tombs he found more
and more of the same: exquisite treasures and the bodies of

servants and courtiers and guards, all almost beyond count. In every case the bodies were dressed in the most elaborate costumes and jewelry, the women in gold and silver headdresses and necklaces and bracelets, the men armed with golden weapons. The king's tomb had been robbed and his body was gone, but the queen's was found intact, her body even more elaborately swathed in gold and jewels than those of her attendants—gold in pendants and chains, inlaid with mosaics of jewels, reaching down to her waist; ribbons of gold around her hair (she seems to have worn a great wig); gold pins and bracelets, all in a magnificently wrought art.

The bodies of the sixty-eight women—they were accompanied by six menservants—were a mystery that Woolley could not easily explain. The women, and the men, seemed to have died willingly—there were no signs that they had been killed either outside or inside the tomb.

> It is most probable that the victims walked to their places, took some kind of drug—opium or hashish would serve— and lay down in order; after the drug had worked, whether it produced sleep or death, the last touches were given to their bodies, and the pit was filled in. There does not seem to have been anything brutal in the manner of their deaths.

Sumer's influence extended far over the ancient world, past the Semitic lands of upper Mesopotamia, the Mediterranean coast, and the Arabian peninsula to Iran, Egypt, and India. The contents of the tombs illustrate a very highly developed state of society. It was an urban civilization in which the architect was familiar with all the basic principles of building known to us today, the artist possessed the highest skills and standards of excellence, and the metal worker had a knowledge of metallurgy and technical skill which few ancient peoples

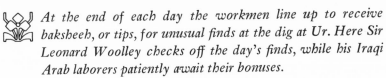 At the end of each day the workmen line up to receive *baksheeh, or tips, for unusual finds at the dig at* Ur. Here Sir *Leonard Woolley checks off the day's finds, while his Iraqi Arab laborers patiently await their bonuses.*

ever rivaled. The merchant carried on a far-flung trade, keeping his records in writing; the armed forces were well organized and victorious; and agriculture was productive and prosperous. The great wealth that all this produced enabled the Sumerians—at least those classes which controlled things—to live in luxury.

Ur and its sister cities survived a long time, some twelve hundred years, so far as is known, and probably longer, if their origins are actually as old as some scholars suspect, going back at least to 4000 B.C. The rise and fall of Mesopotamian cities and kingdoms will be a constant theme of the next chapters. The cities of Sumer lost their freedom about 2350 B.C., when a Semitic nomad, Sharrum-kin, overwhelmed them and founded the dynasty of Akkad. The new ruler is better known as Sargon of Akkad. His dynasty lasted two hundred years, until a new wave of invaders came, the Guti, a nomadic tribe from western Iran, and conquered the Akkadians. The Guti did not survive long: The Sumerians rebelled and regained control, experiencing one of their most creative periods, until

 A restoration of the great ziggurat of the Sumerian ruler Ur-Nammu built in honor of the moon-god Nanna. The temple stood originally about seventy feet high, with a shrine on top. The bottom picture shows the ruins, as uncovered by Woolley in the 1920s.

Hammurabi of Babylon conquered virtually all of Mesopotamia in the fifteenth century B.C. After that Sumer merged
into the general history of Mesopotamia, rising and falling according to the fortunes of invaders, rebels, and dynasties. Ur,
though long gone in the dusts of history, was known to the
West because it was from here that the patriarch Abraham set
forth with his wife Sarah and his flocks and kinsmen to go to
the land of Canaan. The Bible refers to Ur as the city of the
"Chaldeans," but it was Sumer where Abraham was born and
raised, following the calling of a nomadic herdsman, sometime earlier than 1700 B.C. The great Ur finally faded away,
being in a back part of a kingdom that was losing its importance, for at some unknown time the Euphrates River wandered away from the city (it is now ten miles distant from the
ruins), and Ur lost its shipping trade. By 550 B.C. nearly eight
feet of rubbish had accumulated over the court and chambers
of the city's deity, the moon goddess Nin-Gal. Her worship,
under different names, continued, but even though the Babylonian king, Nebuchadnezzar, tried to rebuild the city—he
restored only a small portion—the deities and the people alike
were unable to halt the coming decline. The goddess Nin-Gal
could only lament:

> In the rivers of my city dust has gathered,
>   truly they have been made into holes for the foxes.
> In the fields of the city there is no more grain,
>   the farmer has gone away. . . .
> My palm groves and vineyards that abounded with honey
>   and wine have brought forth the mountain thorn.
> Woe is me, my house is a ruined stable.
> I am the herdsman whose cattle have been scattered.
> I am an exile from the city, that has found no rest.
> I am a stranger dwelling in a strange city.

6

BABYLON,
NEXT TO NINEVEH

IN THE FIRST HALF OF THE LAST MILLENNIUM BEFORE CHRIST
the two cities of Nineveh and Babylon stood above the other
cities of Mesopotamia in importance. They were the centers
of rival empires, rising and falling according to the whims of
their respective rulers and the fortunes of war. It was an un-
relieved period of troubles, of clashes between great empires,
and attacks by nomads and barbarians who seemed to appear
on all sides, hard, restless people who steadily nibbled away at
the fringes of the Assyrian and Babylonian lands, as the two
nations, with the third power of Egypt constantly challenged,
threatened and fought each other.

Nineveh was an old city, dating back to the end of the third
millennium B.C., many times allowed to go into a decline, many
times rebuilt, often a capital, even though newly installed kings
had a habit of starting afresh with new cities. Somehow Nineveh seemed to attract the kings as the ideal capital.

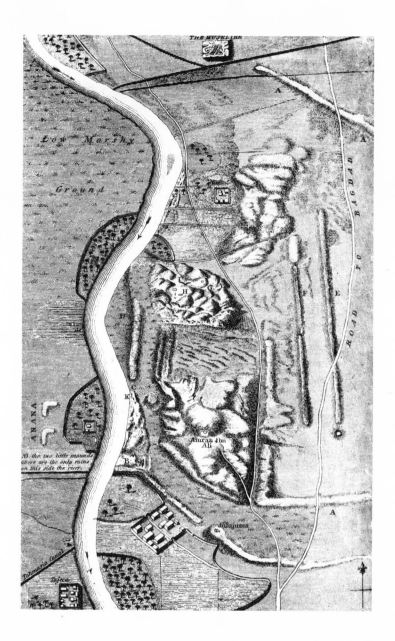

 A nineteenth-century map of Babylon shows the important buildings, with the river Euphrates running through the center of the city. The river had an unfortunate tendency to wander, as did its partner, the Tigris, and sometimes the city would be left dry; other times the Tigris would move westward, and create huge swamps along Babylon's outer suburbs.

Babylon was as old, or even older. Its proper name was Babilu, the "Gate of the Gods"; we use the Greek version. It was probably here that the famous Tower of Babel, or Bab-il, the "Gate of the God," was constructed. It was a ziggurat, the common sacred tower of the Sumerian city. But in this case, according to the Book of Genesis, the builders were scattered about the earth and their language confused so that they could not understand each other's speech, probably a reference to the difficulties that the Sumerians and the latter Semitic peoples had in understanding each other's languages. In this last millennium, after passing through many hands and many phases of prosperity and decline, Babylonia, the southern part of Mesopotamia, the old Sumeria, was taken over by a people called the Kaldi, or Chaldeans, noted not only for their ferocity in war but their intellectual pursuits, including the art and science of astrology.

In the ninth century B.C. the Assyrians, who were expanding their rule in all directions, made a special effort against the small Semitic kingdoms along the Mediterranean, usually each other's hostile neighbors. In 853 the Assyrians defeated the combined forces of Syria and Samaria, the latter led by Ahab, and with this victory behind them were able to impose tributes on the various kings of Israel. In the late eighth century Assyria, under King Shalmaneser V (727–722), threatened Israel again and forced it to pay tribute as vassals. Hosea, the king of Israel, turned to the Egyptians for aid. The Assyrian king considered this an act of treachery and had Hosea arrested and imprisoned. Shalmaneser died before events could move further, but his successor, Sargon II, invaded Israel and the surrounding lands, including Samaria, and inflicted a disastrous defeat upon the people of Israel. Sargon, according to the Assyrians' own records, deported 27,290 of the elite of Israel, settling them in Mesopotamia and Persia, as far away as Elam, where many found homes in the old city of Susa. In the Bible the Israelites attribute their disastrous defeat not to the superiority of Assyrian arms but to the fact that:

> the people of Israel did secretly against the Lord their God things that were not right. . . . And they did wicked things, provoking the Lord to anger, and they served idols.

The Israelites had worshiped molten images of two calves—the bull and the cow were ancient sacred objects—and had practiced human sacrifices, burning "their sons and daughters as offerings." They also practiced divination and sorcery. Therefore "the Lord removed Israel out of His sight" into Assyria.

The inhabitants of Samaria were also deported, and other tribes were displaced from the borderlands of Assyria and settled there. These are the people later and now known as Samaritans. Because these wild nomads did not know "the law of the god of the land" they were punished with attacks by lions. Therefore they petitioned to have a Jewish priest sent to teach them the law. Despite their willing conversion the Jews did not consider the Samaritans true in the worship of the Lord their God.

Sargon's successor was his son, Sennacherib, not only a great and feared warrior but a builder as well. Sennacherib extended the Assyrian kingdom into Persia on the east and attacked the northernmost cities of Babylonia, the traditional enemy. He also renewed the campaigns against the people of Palestine. Sennacherib took many of the fortified cities of Judah, and finally attacked Jerusalem. It was here that the Assyrians were brought to a halt, an event of which we have an account from the defenders themselves, for the Prophet Isaiah wrote:

Thus says the Lord concerning the king of Assyria: He shall not come into this city, or shoot an arrow there, or come before it with a shield, or cast up a siege mound against it. . . . And the angel of the Lord went forth, and slew a hundred and eighty-five thousand in the camp of the Assyrians; and when men arose early in the morning, behold, these were all dead bodies. Then Sennacherib, king of Assyria departed, and went home and dwelt in Nineveh.

It was apparently a plague that had struck down the Assyrian army. Sennacherib continued his wars, sparing the people of Judah, but invading Armenia. A major undertaking, however, was not his continual warfare but the rebuilding of Nineveh into one of the most beautiful cities of Mesopotamia. New streets were cut, public squares enlarged, water courses and canals dug, or revised, and stone flood defenses erected to protect the palace against the customary rising of the Tigris in spring. The king's palace, a new one, was centered in a great park patterned after "Mount Amanus, wherein were set all kinds of plants and fruit trees such as grow in the mountains and in Chaldea." Beyond the royal garden were vast orchards, irrigated by a new canal six miles long; the king soon added more gardens of botanicals, of "all the plants of the land of Syria, myrrh plants, whose luxuriance was greater than in their native habitat, and all kinds of mountain vines." He created an artificial marshland, which he stocked with water birds, wild pigs, and deer, a replica of the natural swamps of the delta of the far south. He was something of a scientist, too, and experimented with new methods of metallurgy and new techniques of casting.

I, Sennacherib, through the acute intelligence which the noble god Ea had granted me and with my own experiment-

ing, achieved the casting of bronze colossal lions open at the
knee, which no king before me had done. . . . Over great
posts and palm-trunks I built a clay mould for twelve colossal lions together with twelve colossal bulls . . . and poured
bronze therein as in casting half-shekel pieces.

Like so many of the other Mesopotamian kings he was an interesting, inventive man. But one must not forget that his
magnificent works—his gardens, palace, public parks, waterways, and aqueducts—were constructed by slave labor, or by
subjects pressed into work. And his enemies were commonly
blinded, burned, flayed alive, or beheaded.

Sennacherib's constant preoccupation was with the Babylonians, or Chaldeans, with whom he and his predecessors had
fought over and over again. In 689 B.C. Sennacherib made a
final assault on the capital city itself, determined to erase from
the memory of mankind the name of this hated rival in power,
influence, and beauty (for Babylon was probably the most
famous city of the time). The attack was one of the most
brutal in ancient history. All the inhabitants were slaughtered,
their bodies heaped in the streets in such great piles that the
Assyrian troops had difficulty in passing by. Houses were
pulled down and leveled. Even the temples were not spared,
some being toppled into the canals. Then the canals were
broken apart and the banks of the Euphrates and the dykes
and levees that had protected the city were destroyed so that
the river waters poured into the city, inundating everything.
As a final symbolic gesture earth from Babylon's streets, now
mud, was loaded on barges and taken to faraway Dilmun,
where it was dumped into the ocean to be carried off by the
currents to the ends of the earth. Now, like a man recovering
from a fever—for it was a fever of madness—Sennacherib
turned to peaceful affairs. To please a favorite wife, Nakiya,

 *A massive winged bull was one of the amazing objects dis-
covered by the adventurous and persistent Austen Henry
Layard at the palace of Nimrud in northern Mesopotamia.
Among his finds were a winged bull and a winged lion eventually sent to the Metropolitan Museum of Art in New York.*

he let her name one of her children, a younger son of the many
he had borne by his various wives, as his successor. But in 681
the boy's older half-brothers, resenting this insult, attacked
their father as he was praying in the great temple of Nineveh,
beating him to death with a golden statue.

A generation passed. Babylon, now Assyrian, was rebuilt
by the conquerors. Nakiya, now a grandmother, was happy
to see her two grandsons on the two greatest thrones of the
world, Ashurbanipal at Nineveh, his brother Shamash-shum-
ukin at Babylon. Events were moving rapidly for the two
kingdoms. Not only were the nomads causing endless troubles,
but the Egyptians were driving Assyrian garrisons out of their
land; and on the highlands and mountains of Iran the Elamites,
and after them their cousins, the Medes and the Persians, were
testing Assyrian strength. The kingdom of Babylonia, reduced
to the city ọf Babylon, alone, under Shamash-shum-ukin, became involved in a confusing situation among Nineveh, Elam,
and the Chaldeans, turning against the Assyrians of Nineveh.
Ashurbanipal attacked his brother in Babylon, who could not
get any support from his allies, the Elamites. Babylon was
blockaded, and famine set in, reaching the point where the defenders resorted to cannibalism. In 648 B.C. Babylon surrendered. To escape the humiliation that comes to defeated kings,
Shamash-shum-ukin set fire to his palace and threw himself
into the flames. The rebel Assyrian generals and officers were
hunted down and killed, and their corpses cut up and "fed to
the dogs, the swine, the wolves, the vultures, the birds of
heaven, and the fish of the deep."

It was but a question of time before the Assyrians were
forced off the historical scene. With the capture of Nineveh
in 612 the Chaldeans, or Neo-Babylonians, dominated the
stage, having forced the Medes as well into the background.

War with Egypt, which controlled land as far north as Syria, was now inevitable. The new Babylonian general, Nebuchadnezzar, made a frontal attack on the powerful Egyptian forces at Carcamesh, in Syria, in 605. An interested observer, the Prophet Jeremiah, noted "the mighty man hath stumbled against the mighty, they are fallen both of them together," for the casualties on each side were tremendous. The Egyptians fled in fear.

> They are dismayed and have turned backward.
> Their warriors are beaten down,
>   and have fled in haste;
>   they look not back—
>   terror on every side!
> The swift cannot flee away, nor the warrior escape;
>   in the north by the river Euphrates
>   they have stumbled and fallen.

The Egyptian defeat shook the world, for the subjected peoples knew that their one ally was gone. Now they had the full power and fury of the Babylonians to fear. The king of Judah, Jehoiakim, submitted to Nebuchadnezzar, paying him tribute for three years, but then he turned to the Egyptians for help, a move that cost him his life. His son followed his policies, unwise and sinful (according to the prophets), the result being that the Babylonians attacked Jerusalem and carried off the leading people and the treasures of the Temple. The figures of captives in 2 Kings 25 are not clear: One verse refers to ten thousand, another eight thousand. Jeremiah reports 3,023, but this may not include the women and children. At any rate the princes, warriors, craftsmen, and smiths were taken, and "none remained, except the poorest people of the land." The Babylonian captivity had begun.

Three years later the survivors in Jerusalem, under King
Zedekiah, revolted against the Babylonians. The king tried to
enlist the support of the Egyptians, but failed. The Babylonians
besieged and blockaded the city for eighteen months and
finally starved it out, the city falling again in 586 B.C. For his
rashness in challenging the Babylonians, Zedekiah was brought
to Nebuchadnezzar's headquarters to see his sons and court
officials slaughtered, then he was taken to Babylon, blinded,
and led through the customary procession of the vanquished
before finally being executed. Jerusalem was virtually destroyed by the enemy. The Temple, the palace, and all the
houses were burned and the walls pulled down. The Babylonian soldiers looted the city, taking away the treasures of the
Temple, the gold and silver, the bronze pillars, the incense
dishes, and the ceremonial utensils. In this second capture of
Jerusalem the Babylonians deported a mere 832 people, according to Jeremiah 52. Yet elsewhere the total figure is given
as 4,800. Whatever the number, it was another blow to the
Jewish state.

The Prophet renders a harsh judgment upon Jerusalem's
king Zedekiah and the people for their sins.

> He did what was evil in the sight of the Lord his God.
> He did not humble himself before Jeremiah the prophet,
>   who spoke from the mouth of the Lord.
> He also rebelled against King Nebuchadnezzar. . . .
> All the leading priests and the people were likewise
>   exceedingly unfaithful,
>   following all the abominations of the nations. . . .

The exiles were forced into a complete reappraisal of their
way of life and a radical rethinking of their roles in the world
and particularly of their God and His plan for them and how

they were to respond to it. Many could not believe the exile
would last more than a short while, but others apparently favored a complete integration into Babylon. Jeremiah sent the
exiles a letter about what to do, speaking on behalf of the Lord
their God.

> Build houses and live in them;
>   plant gardens and eat their produce.
> Take wives and have sons and daughters;
>   take wives for your sons,
>   and give your daughters in marriage,
>   that they may bear sons and daughters;
>   multiply there and do not decrease.
> But seek the welfare of the city
>   where I have sent you for exile,
>   and pray to the Lord on its behalf,
>   for in its welfare you will find your welfare.

He warns them not to let false prophets and diviners deceive
them into thinking return is imminent, for:

> Thus says the Lord:
> When seventy years are completed for Babylon,
> I will visit you, and I will fulfill to you my promise
>   and bring you back to this place.

A number of the exiles prospered, and some entered into the
service of the Babylonians, and later the Persians. The Book
of Daniel, which was written perhaps three centuries after the
exile and may be either a retelling of an ancient tradition or a
story meant merely to edify, tells how four young men—
Daniel and his three companions, Shadrach, Meshach, and
Abed-nego—were taken directly into Nebuchadnezzar's
household. Daniel would not defile himself by eating the pro-

 Not all the Jews exiled to Babylon returned home after Cyrus released them from captivity. However, the founding of the state of Israel brought many of the descendants of the exiles back to the Holy Land. This is a Persian Jew newly come to Jerusalem; he is caretaker of the Persian synagogue.

hibited foods served at the royal table, but he redeemed himself by correctly interpreting the king's dreams, for which he was made governor over the whole province of Babylonia and chief prefect over the wise men, diviners, magicians, and astrologers, a most important post, for the Chaldeans of Babylon were heavily involved in the occult. Daniel made his three companions his deputies in the province, preferring to remain at the court himself. The exiles fulfilled the injunction to multiply their numbers. A century later the few thousand original deportees had reached a figure of some 150,000. Yet there were a number who were unhappy, despite their success in Babylon. One of the most poignant of the psalms emphasizes the separation from their homeland.

> By the waters of Babylon,
> there we sat down and wept
>   when we remembered Zion.
> On the willows there
>   we hung up our lyres.
> For there our captors
>   required of us songs,
> and our tormentors, mirth, saying,
>   "Sing us one of the songs of Zion!"
> How shall we sing the Lord's song in a foreign land?
> If I forget you, O Jerusalem,
>   let my right hand wither!
> Let my tongue cleave to the roof of my mouth,
>   if I do not set Jerusalem above my highest joy!

While the Neo-Babylonians were warring with the small kingdoms of the eastern Mediterranean shore, a new figure appeared in the mountains of Iran, a man who was to effect radical changes in the Middle East. He was Cyrus, a Persian, who by 560 B.C. had taken over all of Iran as far north as the Caspian

Sea, overrunning the Medes and incorporating them into his kingdom. With his armies ever-increasing due to his victories—he took under his command the armies of the vanquished—he descended to the northern Mesopotamian plain, capturing Syria and the upper regions of the Tigris and Euphrates. Now in 539 B.C. he was able to attack Babylon.

Conditions in what was left of the empire were not good. Nebuchadnezzar had died, leaving behind a vacuum, which was filled by an inept general, Nabua'id, who had been victorious over an army of Medes in Syria, but who was not sensitive to the demands of the people of Babylon. Nabua'id enraged the priesthood and the populace by attempting to replace the city's deity, Marduk, whose cult was centered around a gold statue eighteen feet high, with the Syrian moon god Sin. When the Persians overran what was left of the Babylonian empire and had surrounded the city, resistance to them was unusually light. An inscription found on a Babylonian artifact, a seal called the Cyrus Cylinder, tells how the Babylonians looked to their conqueror.

> Marduk . . . sought a righteous prince after his own heart, whom he took by the hand. Cyrus, King of Anshan [Persia], he called by name, to lordship over the whole world he appointed him. . . . To his city Babylon he caused him to go . . . going as a friend and companion at his side. . . . Without battle and conflict he permitted him to enter Babylon. He spared the city a calamity.

The Jews also saw Cyrus in a divine light. The "Second" Isaiah states that the Lord says of Cyrus, "He is my shepherd, and he shall fulfill my purpose," which is the rebuilding of the Temple. And—

> Thus says the Lord to his anointed, to Cyrus,

> whose right hand I have grasped,
> to subdue nations before him
> and ungird the lions of kings,
> to open doors before him
> that gates may not be closed.

Cyrus returned to the Jews the treasures that Nebuchadnezzar had taken from the Temple, and he released the Jews from captivity so that they could return to their homeland.

> The Lord, the God of heaven, has given me all the kingdoms
> of the earth.
> And he has charged me to build him a house at Jerusalem,
> which is in Judah.
> Whoever is among you of all his people,
> may the Lord his God be with him.
> Let him go up.

Some forty-two thousand left immediately for Jerusalem, one of their purposes being to rebuild the Temple, but local opposition forced the returnees to abandon their plans. Under other Persian kings, over the next century, more Jews left Babylon for their homeland, but still a sizable group remained, having become adjusted to the lenient rule of the Persians.

The Persians could not be stopped: Their armies soon took all the Mesopotamian plain and beyond. Theirs was an enlightened but still despotic rule. Unlike the Assyrians Cyrus did not deport entire populations, an act which disrupted the economic progress of the empire for the temporary benefit of the central government. In the long run having wealthy satraps, as the Persians called their provinces, provided a steady income through taxation. Trade routes long dormant because of the incessant warfare of the past were reopened. Trade was car-

ried on as faraway as China by an overland route; silk was an
important item. A royal road was built from Susa, for a while
the capital, in the Iranian hill country overlooking Mesopotamia, along the east bank of the Tigris, running north to Cappadocia and across to Sardis near the Aegean. At its height
the empire reached from the estuaries of the Indus River system in the east to the Danube in Europe, from the frontiers of
China to North Africa. Even parts of Greece were included,
for the Greek cities of Asia Minor either were conquered or
submitted, as did many on the Hellenic mainland. Only Sparta
and Athens were able to remain free. But Cyrus did not plun-
der the Greek cities, nor those of the other small city-states.
He treated the famed Croesus, the last ruler of Lydia, with
kindness and respect, once Cyrus had come to realize the
cruelty of the punishment he was imposing on his smaller
rival.

Croesus had taken over Sardis in 560 B.C., subduing the
Greek cities; he was content to rule through Greek "tyrannoi"
susceptible to his wishes. Cyrus, who was building his own
empire at the same time, could not bear having a powerful
ruler on his northern flank. Lydians and Persians had already
battled once, the predecessors of both kings having opposed
each other in what promised to be a fight to the death. But at
the height of the battle an eclipse of the sun had taken place,
and both armies had run in panic.

Croesus, seeing the Persians advance again, went to the oracle at Delphi, who was consulted not only by Greeks but by
barbarians like Croesus. The oracle told Croesus that if he
crossed the river Halys, the boundary line between Lydia and
the oncoming Persians, a great kingdom would fall. Unfortunately Croesus forgot to ask which kingdom, for when he
forded the river to attack the enemy, it was his army, not Cy-

rus's, which lost the battle. With this victory in 548 B.C. the Persians had reached the Aegean.

Cyrus took Croesus alive and placed him on a mighty funeral pyre. The Greeks, who speculated about this incident involving two enemies, did not know whether Cyrus was fulfilling a vow or enjoying the usual victory sacrifice (human sacrifices were still all too common), or merely testing the gods to see if they would save Croesus, who had the reputation of being an unusually religious man. With the flames leaping about him Croesus called out the name of his conqueror, more it seems as a prayer than a supplication. Again he called, or chanted, and a third time. It now came to Cyrus that he was being abominably cruel to a vanquished foe. He ordered the flames put out, but at this point the fire was beyond control. Having lost hope in Cyrus, Croesus prayed to the Greek god Apollo, for he had been unusually generous to the god's cult. Out of a clear sky clouds appeared, which produced a torrent of rain, and the fire was extinguished. Thereafter Cyrus and Croesus became very close friends.

Perhaps the incident with Croesus taught Cyrus some kind of lesson, for when he took Babylon, the biggest, richest, and most famous city in the world, he did not allow it to be sacked or looted, even sparing the temples, which proclaimed a paganism that he personally must have abhorred. The Persian followed the religion of Ahura Mazda, the One Supreme Lord proclaimed by the Iranian Prophet Zoroaster, who lived roughly 626 to 551 B.C. (the exact dates are a matter of dispute). Cyrus, for matters of state, not only did not actively interfere with the Babylonians' beliefs, but for a while actually encouraged them. He had his son Cambyses officiate at the Babylonian celebration of the new year, a most important festival, for it was centered around Marduk. The god, or his priests, invested the young Persian prince, though a foreigner, with kingship, an act with a twofold significance, for it proclaimed that from here on the Persian royal family was both temporal and spiritual ruler over Mesopotamia. With this rite a foreign nation had become accepted as sovereign over the lands of the Tigris and Euphrates. It was the first time since the Sumerians, mysterious and unknown in origin, had founded their city-states over three thousand years earlier. The rulers and people succeeding the Sumerians had been members of various indigenous peoples, mainly Semitic. Except for some fringe lands temporarily held by outsiders, notably the Egyptians, the rule, conquest, and reconquest of Mesopotamia had been a family affair of peoples of the steppes, desert, and lowlands surrounding the two rivers and their waterways and delta.

But the Persians brought more than foreign blood: They brought a foreign idea, their religion, that was powerful and persuasive, and formed a direct challenge to the multiplicity of deities, great and small, that had populated both the city temples and the Mesopotamian countryside. Moreover Ahura Mazda was a loving god, whose favor was gained not by sacrifices of beasts and men, or burned offerings or propitiations, but by a life honestly and correctly lived. Whether or not the Zoroastrians—for the followers of Ahura Mazda were named after the Prophet—followed the true faith literally is not the point: They had the ideal set before them, and it was each man's own responsibility to practice it. No great work such as the building of a magnificent temple, or the immolation of war captives, would gain favor with Ahura Mazda; only one's own life lived in an atmosphere of love and generosity could be sufficient.

I must digress for a moment about Ahura Mazda and Zoroastrianism, because the faith was to affect the events for all

 The winged disk of Ahura Mazda, the Supreme Lord of Zoroastrianism (and the ancient Iranian version of the Jehovah of the Jews and Christians, and of the Muslims' Allah) surmounts winged figures of demigods symbolizing the deified rulers of the Achaeminid dynasty. In Zoroastrianism, Ahura Mazda is the One, "God without a predecessor," the Omniscient Source of Existence, and the Divine Will.

time, its doctrines being absorbed by the Jews and later the Christians and the Arabs. Some basic points:

Ahura Mazda created the universe, the purpose being the bliss and welfare of mankind. All of creation is bound by the laws of growth and destruction. The might and power of Ahura Mazda have two forms. One, Spenta Mainyu, prospers and maintains everything. The other, Anra Mainyu, destroys. These two forces are also light and dark, in short, truth and the lie. Beyond these two forms are others, helpers in the divine plan, various powers of nature, of the mind, of thought, angels and archangels helping mankind to gain the blissful light of Ahura Mazda.

But only Ahura Mazda is omnipotent, omniscient, omnipresent—eternal. In the end Anra Mainyu, the power of the lie, limited in time, power, and knowledge, will be annihilated with his wicked cohorts, and all evil will be extirpated, while mankind will be resurrected and the world renovated.

Man is composed of a body and a soul, which are teamed with a kind of supernatural guide, the *fravashi*. Man also has a vital breath, and the faculties of discernment and conscience. Man must strive to lead a good life, to avoid evil in order to be saved. There will be a last judgment, with each individual to go to a heaven or a hell or an intermediate state, and a resurrection of the dead. Zoroastrianism also taught a Satan and a hero-saviour, a messiah, to come. At the time of the exile Judaism was still in a formative state. Only upon the return to the Holy City were the books of the Pentateuch, or Old Testament, edited and written out in final form. Many of the primary concepts of Judaism (and hence Christianity and Islam) date from the period of Persian influence.

The doctrines of Zoroastrianism were expressed in a massive scripture, the Avesta, composed partly by the Prophet, partly by his disciples. There were believed to be two master copies of the work—it was said to be about ten times the size of the Bible—written down some time after the Prophet's death, for initially it had been passed on orally. Both copies were written in gold ink on ox hides; one was kept at Persepolis, the other at Samarkand. Alexander the Great is said to have destroyed both, an act for which Zoroastrians revile his memory.

The doctrine of Zoroastrianism, of the One Supreme Lord, was spread throughout the Persian empire. The Persians did not seem to be active proselytizers, but the people they conquered were receptive to their religious ideas and were willing to replace the pantheons of wrathful, angry deities, punitive and irrational, who could not be loved but only appeased, by an all-loving Lord. This concept of the single God, to that point held only by the Jews, was one that opened the way for Christianity and Islam and all their varied heresies.

Persian rule expanded, pacifying, taxing. Cyrus's dynasty, known as Achaeminid, grew in size and wealth, luxury and opulence. It required considerable income and so it overtaxed its many far-flung and varied subjects. The Babylonians, who had welcomed Cyrus, revolted against his grandson Xerxes in 482 B.C. The Persians quickly retook the city and tore down part of the great walls to keep the city defenseless in the future. Xerxes is also said—but this has never been proven—to have destroyed the leading temples. What is known is that the great golden statue of Marduk was taken to the Persian capital at Parsargadae and melted down for the royal treasury. If the Persians did not destroy the Babylonian temples—at this point they had no interest in maintaining gods they did not respect, in fact, knew did not exist—they apparently taxed the buildings so heavily the priests could no longer keep them up, and if mud brick, whether raw or baked, is not constantly attended

to, it disintegrates. That the Persians might have been moti-
vated by religious prejudice against pagan gods is shown by
the fact that the early emperors consistently encouraged the
exiled Jews to return home and reconstruct the Temple of the
One Lord. Besides the initial offer by Cyrus in 538 B.C. Darius I encouraged Zerubbabel and Joshua to lead another group
to their homeland, as did Artaxerxes I, who sent Nehemiah, a
Jew who was a high official in the Persian court, and after him
Artaxerxes II, who gave Ezra a commission granting him religious authority over those who practiced Judaism in and
around Judea. Artaxerxes also financed the exiles with a sub-
stantial subsidy in gold and in sacred utensils for their work,
and promised more whenever it was needed.

During its entire reign the Achaemenid dynasty was successful in its military ventures and its ability to keep a wide
assortment of unruly peoples, from India to Lydia, fairly
peaceful, considering the vast territory. Only the Greeks were
difficult, though even with them the Persians had better results
than could be expected. They ruled the Greek cities of Asia
Minor and even most of those on the Greek mainland, except
for those two intransigent small states of Sparta and Athens.
The Athenians had watched from a distance, having had to
abandon their city for a short while, while the Persians sacked
Athens, burned down its heart, and destroyed the temples of
the Acropolis. The two allies finally defeated the Persians,
though their enemy's army included a large number of Greek
troops who fought bravely.

It soon came the turn of the Greeks to take on Persia, for
after nearly two centuries of easy rule the empire had not only
grown too fat and soft, but was overextended and becoming
cruel. The Greeks who conquered the Persians were actually
Macedonians under Alexander the Great, people whom the

average Greek considered up-country rustics, though Alexander's family claimed descent from the great Achilles, hero of the Trojan War, and beyond him, from the god Zeus himself. Greece had always been a land of neighbors, brothers, and friends warring against each other: In 359 Philip, Alexander's father, having seized power in the usual bloody massacre of relatives, began to attack other Greek states with considerable success, for he had several strengths to draw upon. One was ample manpower in a very feudal society, in which people were bound with fierce loyalty to their leader. The second was a new gold mine which meant steady pay for his troops. The third was the ingenious invention of the phalanx, a group of infantrymen armed with long spears, each man in the first five rows having a progressively longer one, so that all, when pointed forward, formed an impenetrable and formidable weapon. Philip began to lop off one Greek city after another. The Greeks awoke to the danger too late, though the famed orator Demosthenes had unsuccessfully warned long and loud about the new enemy.

Philip knew Greece well. He had been in many of the cities, and he understood the weaknesses of the people and their strengths (he had the best Greek tutors for his son, among them the philosopher Aristotle). And he knew when and where to strike. But to Philip's credit, though he could be a harsh victor, he also had a purpose in mind. He wanted the disorganized, competitive Greek states to form a unit, to stay at peace with each other, and so he established a general assembly of the Greeks. He then called for this Hellenic League to join with Macedonia in a general war against Persia, to free the Greeks of Asia Minor. At this point he was murdered.

Alexander, then twenty, took over. If the young general had been just another Macedonian princeling, the Greeks might have regained the initiative and freed themselves of the alliance. But Alexander was one of the military and political geniuses of world history. In a series of rapid moves over fifteen months he stamped out incipient rebellions, marched as far north as the Danube to protect that flank, and then when Thebes, one of the leading Greek cities, received a bribe from Persia to attack the Macedonians, Alexander marched a second time into Greece and thoroughly destroyed all opposition. Now he was ready for Asia and the Persians, who were led by another Darius, the third of that name. But Darius, though of heroic size (six and a half feet) and impressive mien, was a weak and luxury-loving monarch, with little understanding of war.

With 40,000 men Alexander invaded Cappadocia, that part of Asia Minor directly opposite Greece, and marched east and south to the point where the Phoenician coastline meets Cappadocia. Here there is a small but beautiful port town, Issus, where it was clear there would be a major battle with Darius, who had not yet engaged in any battles with Alexander. In 333 B.C. the rulers of the two most formidable powers of that period were to meet face to face in battle.

The Persians, thinking they had cut off the Greeks, who were still inland, took over the port town, where they found some Greeks wounded. Darius ordered them cut up alive.

The battle was soon joined, the small forces of the Macedonians easily overcoming the greater armies of the Persians by means of the phalanx, a fighting tool so fierce that the Persians turned and fled, led by Darius himself; impressive as he was in his chariot, the king was a weakling in combat. He left behind, in the supposed safety of Issus, all the women of the royal family waiting for him in a magnificent tent with a victory banquet prepared. The Greeks ate the meal that night and kept the gold and silver utensils. Darius abandoned his chariot and escaped on relays of horses, finding safety only on the east shore of the Euphrates.

Alexander spared the king's women, though it was expected by both victor and vanquished that they were his privilege. This generous act gained him the respect of the ordinary people among the conquered and the recognition on the part of the Persian nobles that they were facing someone unusual. But he was not so sparing of the harems left behind by the enemy generals who lost at Issus. Darius, in safety, sent Alexander a request to ransom his family, but at the same time blamed the current war on Philip, whom he accused of breaking a treaty.

Alexander now moved down the Mediterranean coast, taking over the small kingdoms and city-states the Persians had ruled for so long, installing his own pro-Greek kings and governors. His campaign, with some hard battles, continued into Egypt, which he took easily, for the people welcomed deliverance from the Persians. The Egyptians hailed him as both king and god, the deified warrior who had saved them. Alexander did not discourage this cult of divinization, which also appeared among other conquered peoples. He toured Egypt, seeing the pyramids and other antiquities and the great cities, bigger than anything the Macedonian had ever imagined existed. On his tour of Egypt he founded the city which bears his name, Alexandria (he was to found twenty-five in all), walking about with his engineers and architects, laying out the sites of palaces and temples for both the Greek and the Egyptian gods.

With the conquest of Egypt, Alexander was no longer the petty prince of a backward mountain state but a world ruler. Now when he moved, it was with a vast retinue, an army of soldiers, of camp followers, administrators, historians, astrologers and diviners, engineers, women, and slaves. Many of the soldiers had wives and children, others had local women they had taken, and everyone had slaves. With each victory Alexander's entourage grew.

In July, 331, he invaded Mesopotamia. Darius III was waiting for him beyond the Tigris, on the plain of Gaugamela, with a vast army from all the Persian satrapies, including India, which furnished a contingent of elephants. But instead of heading directly across the burning desert sands toward Darius in the middle of summer, which would have exhausted his troops, Alexander took a route along the cooler mountains and highlands, not turning south until he had crossed the Tigris. Meanwhile Darius, in anticipation of the Greeks, had a huge battleground prepared, the earth being leveled so his chariots could maneuver freely. From his vantage point above the plain Alexander could see the Persians. He had 40,000 infantry and 7,000 cavalry. The Persians numbered 200,000 infantry and 20,000 horses, plus the elephants. Alexander gave his troops four days' rest while he and his generals worked out their battle plans. Considering the Persian superiority it seemed logical to strike at night, but Alexander overruled this suggestion.

Darius, with his superiority of five to one, tried to outguess the Greeks. He assumed the logical—a night attack—and all night long his troops waited. At dawn, with the Persians exhausted from lack of sleep, the Greeks attacked.

The Persian army was drawn up on a long line to outflank the Greeks by superior numbers. In an apparent attempt to outflank the Persian overlap Alexander moved some of his troops further to the right. The Persians moved theirs, and Alexander went even further. The Persians saw they had been maneuvered onto rough ground, so to keep the Greeks from moving even further onto difficult land they attacked. The

Persian center had become thinner and weaker than it should have been, and right in that center was Darius himself, tall and impressive in his armor, the perfection of royalty at war. With a loud cry the Greek cavalry drove straight into the center directly at the royal chariot.

A British military historian, E. W. Marsden, who studied the battle of Gaugamela, states some of the problems involved in a battle in antiquity.

> It is difficult to re-create the chaos characteristic of full-scale engagements at certain stages, the confusion caused by noise, movement, and dust, the atmosphere of doubt and uncertainty, the horrible carnage. . . . It must be extraordinarily difficult for modern generals to remain calm and detached when controlling operations in a command post some miles from the scene of the fighting. How much harder it would be for Alexander and Darius, who were stationed in the line of battle itself! Darius appears not to have possessed the rare ability to sift conflicting reports, to make correct observations, and, remaining cool and unflurried, to issue swift and well-considered orders in such circumstances. Alexander had this ability in a pronounced degree.

With the Greeks breaking through his center, Darius, now on the defensive and not the attack, turned and fled as he had at Issus. But the Persians, having superior numbers, did not quit but fought on. Alexander, committed to the battle, could not pursue his royal enemy as he had wished. When the Greeks were able to follow, with the Persians routed, they found that Darius again had abandoned his chariot. He fled north, through Kurdistan and into Armenia, where he had a summer palace, to try to regroup his shattered armies. The way south along the Tigris, to Babylon, and beyond that, to Susa and Persepolis, was open to the Greeks. Alexander had captured Mesopotamia.

Besides oil, the Middle East also possesses underground energy in the form of thermal springs deep within the earth. The same techniques of drilling are used to release thermal energy. It is used to power electrical plants, and to heat homes, factories, and offices. Thermal springs are found throughout the Fertile Crescent.

Now he entered Babylon, having decided that the city was more important than the pursuit of an emperor failed. Babylon was open and undefended, its hundred gates welcoming the Greeks. The streets were strewn with flowers and incensed with rare scents. Alexander was given a chariot of solid gold for his victory procession. Though the Babylonians had once welcomed the Persians, now they hated them, and instead they welcomed the conquerors of their enemies. But what was most important to Alexander was the royal treasury, intact and untouched. With the treasuries he had picked up earlier in Cappadocia, Egypt, and Syria—the old city of Damascus, a Persian satrap, had provided an unusual amount of loot—he was not only able to pay his troops bonuses and give some home leave (his men were the highest paid of all armies, most of which had to survive on booty), but he had ample funds for further campaigns. The Persians' gold and silver went into his mints, pouring out literally by the ton in the form of coins bearing his image. Everyone had money, and the Babylonians grew even richer off the Greek troops.

Then Alexander turned to the next great Persian cities, Susa and Persepolis. Susa was not contested, and here Alexander found gold and silver amounting to some $90,000,000, as it was reckoned in 1931 by a German economist; today the value would be four or five times that. Then he entered the Persian plateau and turned south toward Persepolis. On the road he met a tragic sight, thousands of Greeks from Asia Minor who had been taken prisoners and made into slaves by Darius III. One of the Greek historians wrote:

> All had been mutilated. Some lacked hands, some feet, some ears and noses. They were men who had learned skills and crafts and done well in training; after which their other

extremities had been cut off and they were left only with those on which their work depended.

When the Greeks entered Persepolis, Alexander let his troops run loose, sacking the city and looting as they willed. Alexander, as usual, took the royal treasure, reported to be three times the size of that at Susa. It was after the wild days at Persepolis, when Alexander and his generals were having a farewell party, that the palace was partially burned down and the copy of the Avesta was destroyed.

In his summer palace Darius waited for a third battle. But his generals would not support him in what had to be a disastrous encounter. As the Greeks, after their peaceful winter in Persepolis, marched north to attack Darius, some of his generals tried to assassinate him, but failed to do the job properly. The dying king was left in a wagon. A few of his loyal retainers rushed to Alexander, now only a few miles away, to tell him of the tragedy and to ask his help. Though he rode up to the palace immediately, Alexander could not find the king in time, for there were sixty wagons to be searched. Darius was dead when he was finally located.

On Alexander went, to the ends of the Persian empire and beyond, his troops protesting, for they were tired of war and wanted to return home with their fantastic wealth. Across the worst and wildest lands of Persia they traveled, fighting snows and tribal chiefs. After one encounter with a remote tribe, which was won when Alexander and three hundred men climbed up the face of a cliff at night, in the snow, to surprise a horde of nomads who barred the pass below, the Persians suddenly surrendered and the women gave a welcoming dance. It was here that Alexander found the woman, Roxana, who became his first wife (he had at least two; the exact number is

not known). The route took the Greeks through the formidable peaks and valleys of the Hindu Kush, through Afghanistan and down into the plain of the Indus Valley, where, after
more horrendous battles, the troops refused to continue further—Alexander had the mouth of the Ganges, at the far end
of India, as his goal. The Greeks finally turned about and
headed back to Persia through warm coastal lands. At Susa
Alexander married a Persian princess; a hundred of his generals also took Persian noblewomen as wives, and so did 10,000
of the Greek soldiers. By now Alexander was facing much
dissatisfaction among the Macedonians. Not only was he accepting Persians as officers and troops on an equal basis with
the Greeks, but he was encouraging Persian ways for his people and actively pushing marriages with the enemy. He had
adopted Persian clothing, wearing trousers instead of the short
kilt that the Greeks wore. The top echelons were heavily
Persianized.

The stop at Susa was only temporary. Alexander had decided to make Babylon the capital of his empire, another deci-
sion that irritated the Macedonians. As the great army of
Greeks now approached the old city, Alexander was met by a
strange procession. Outside the city, on the banks of the Tigris,
where a bridge leads to the western bank (the city was entered
from the west, not the east) was a group of Babylonian astrologers and priests of the ancient gods, the old divinities the
Persians had slighted. They drew Alexander aside and whis-
pered that the omens were against him: He should not enter
the city but should return to the east, to Susa perhaps. Alex-
der consulted astrologers and omens when it suited him: Now
he wanted to enter Babylon, for it was to be the center of his
operations. Partially to humor the astrologers and priests, and
possibly partly to break the curse, he did not cross the bridge

but went down the river to enter the city from the east, a task which meant going through marshes and swamps. He was in Babylon but a few months, planning for his next campaign (probably to the western Mediterranean), enlarging Babylon and its harbor on the Tigris, getting his empire in order. On a trip to inspect some water-poor farmland south of Babylon he had to pass through malarial swamps. A few days later he lay deathly ill. Whether he had caught malaria, or some other fever, or had been poisoned, can never be known. Despite his illness he went to parties two nights running. He was in a delirium for nine days, and finally died, on a hot day in June, 323 B.C.

A magnificent coffin of beaten gold was made for the body, which was embalmed with spices. An elaborate hearse, drawn by sixty-four horses, preceded by elephants, and accompanied by Alexander's elite troops, carried the body across Mesopotamia, where crowds wept at every stop, to Alexandria, where it was entombed in a great shrine that was still standing three hundred years later. Finally in 89 B.C. a Greek ruler of Egypt, Ptolomy IX, needing money to pay his troops, melted down the golden sarcophagus.

After Alexander's death his heirs entered the usual bitter and bloody struggle for the empire. His first wife Roxana, then pregnant with the child who was to be known as Alexander IV, had the second wife, Barzine, murdered. Fourteen years later Roxana and Alexander IV were killed. The Macedonian empire fell into three parts, divided among the generals who were more daring and more ruthless than the others. Ptolemy received Egypt; Lysimachus, Macedonia and Thrace; and Seleucus, Media; and other parts fell to minor Greek rulers.

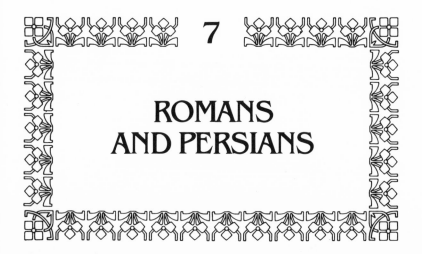

7

ROMANS
AND PERSIANS

PERSIA HAD BEEN CRUSHED BY ALEXANDER, AND HIS DEATH HAD
shattered his own great empire. His ideals, his goals, his ambitions, even his personality, his anima, were assumed by his general, Seleucus, though indifferently. There was only one Alexander; there were many generals, by different names. Seleucus
tried most commendably to impose Greek culture upon the
East, to Hellenize the Iranians and the Mesopotamians. Wars.
Endless forays into other lands. Successes and retreats. We
enter into a period, a long one, for many dynasties, in which
many nations were involved in the struggle over Mesopotamia
and the wealth of the Fertile Crescent. The struggle was—can
one apply that word to a series of dynastic feuds, constant battles, murders, assassinations, and social upheaval highlighted by
passages of great art, city building, and religious innovation?—
dull.

About 305 B.C. Seleucus, determined to regain the Indian satrapy so briefly held by Alexander, followed his predecessor's path across the Hindu Kush and down into India, where he confronted the Indian king Chandragupta Maurya. Where Alexander might have won a province again, Seleucus was lucky to get an impasse. The Indian had 9,000 elephants in his formidable army, and the beasts were but a minor element. Whether there was a battle or not is not known. Seleucus seems to have had second thoughts about a war. At any rate he gave his daughter to Chandragupta in marriage, along with Afghanistan and Baluchistan, which were really not his to dispose of so lightly, and he received in turn 500 elephants, plus, we must assume, wishes of good karma from his new son-in-law. Whatever he received from the Indians worked, for with the help of the 500 elephants he soundly defeated his strongest rival, Antigonus One-Eye, at Ipsus in 301. By the force of their arms— Seleucus was the most skilled and aggressive of Alexander's surviving generals—the Seleucid dynasty, centered in its new capital of Seleucia on the Tigris, at its peak, reached from Afghanistan to the shores of the Bosphorus, leaving the Ptolemies in Egypt and a small section of the Palestine coast, which included Israel.

Seleucus was one of the bridegrooms of Susa, and his dynasty was an equal mixture of Macedonian and Persian blood lines. Like Alexander he had no desire, despite his ancestry, to return to his homeland, for the opulence and the riches of the East were highly attractive. Moreover he had an empire at his disposal, and it was his preoccupation and that of his successors to safeguard the far-flung provinces and dependencies. Greeks and Macedonians were settled everywhere in a vast program of town planning in the hopes of founding a worldwide Hellenized civilization; some of the most important cities of the period were Seleucid, among them Antioch. Greek city-states were founded by later Seleucids as far east as India. The Greeks, in the tradition of Alexander, were fearless in setting off into unknown lands, with only tenuous links to their bases, to found new kingdoms, and there were Greek kings, now virtually nomads, who for centuries wandered here and there with their warriors, still following the ancient traditions of Alexander and the Seleucids, establishing principalities in western India. They were eventually absorbed into the great mass of the subcontinent, losing all identity, so that today Indians have no knowledge of the Greek presence, though the Greek historians reported on their activities. Recently hordes of Greek coins have been found in Afghanistan and northwest India, pieces of exquisite workmanship bearing the names of forgotten nomadic royalty.

The policy of Hellenizing Mesopotamia, Syria, and Iran was only partially successful. In fact many Greeks, set in a sea of foreigners, were eventually Persianized, to the extent that some of the kings, following the worst concepts of Persian royalty, fell into the blasphemy of considering themselves deities as well as rulers. The chaotic affairs of Mesopotamia, with its sometime provinces of Persia and Syria, and its wars and battles for supremacy, in which men of undoubted talents tried to bring this or that section of the Middle East, or the entirety, under a single unified rule, finally came to a climax with the arrival of another nomadic Iranian people known as the Arsacids, after Arsak (or Arsaces), the founder of the dynasty. Also called the Parthians, these people appeared in the area southeast of the Caspian Sea about 250 B.C. Like the Persians under Cyrus the Great, they possessed enough barbaric energies to overrun all of Iran and then conquer Mesopotamia. Like other conquerors, the Arsacids also built a new capital on

the Tigris, this one known as Ctesiphon, near the former capital of Seleucia, and not far from the future site of Baghdad.

The Arsacids had a long rule, from the middle of the third
century B.C. to 224 A.D. The dynasty furnished a number of
notable kings, warriors, patrons of the arts, founders of cities,
and enemies of the Greeks (and later the Romans). But, like
others of the long period that began with the Seleucids and
ended with the decline of the Sassanians in the seventh century
A.D., they are not the kind of people one lingers over, despite
their unusual staying powers. Few historians spend much time
on them: There are other events, other individuals and peoples
of more flair, more dynamism, better movers and shakers of
the earth.

Far to the west of the Fertile Crescent another mighty power
had been at work. Rome was busy turning the Mediterranean
into a Roman lake. Rome had been reluctant to become involved in Greece, but there the warring among the petty kings
was constant, and during the second century B.C. Greece and
her Asia Minor states were taken over. The Roman generals
could look beyond the Aegean and the shores of Asia and see,
there for the taking, the dozens of small kingdoms of Syria
and Palestine and beyond them the effete, turmoil-prone empire of the Persians, now called Arsacids. It was an easy matter for the Romans to see themselves as the successors of the
Greeks, if not of Alexander himself. They could envision an
empire from the offshore islands of western Europe to Persia,
if not beyond. But there were problems to overcome. In the
first century B.C. the Armenian King Tigranes helped himself
to much of upper Mesopotamia. The Arsacids regained it after
a few years of Armenian rule, their rights being guaranteed in
66 B.C. by the Romans, who wanted a stable situation on their
considerably extended eastern flank. However the Romans

 Conquerors come and go, but the hard, demanding life of the villagers continues virtually unchanged no matter who rules.

could not remain free from a war with the Arsacids: Their troops, crossing from Armenia to Syria, violated the treaty and war began with the Persians. The death of Julius Caesar in 44 B.C. ended his planned massive campaign into Mesopotamia and further east. We can speculate that he saw himself gaining permanently what Alexander held briefly. Constant battles between Romans and Persians nevertheless continued, extending the Romans and weakening the Arsacids.

Then events seem to have been quiet for a long time in the century or so following. Of the most importance for the West was the birth of Jesus Christ in 4 B.C. (as the date has been corrected) in a Palestine occupied by the Romans—quiet, or of such steady and monotonous petty warfare that the fluctuations of borders, the deaths of men, women, and children, and even of kings, could go unnoticed. There is almost no historical documentation for this period in Mesopotamia, until the great Roman, the Emperor Marcus Ulpius Traianus, otherwise known as Trajan Optimus (because of his devotion to the well-being of his own people in Italy) invaded Mesopotamia without resistance, taking Arabia in 106 A.D. and then, having annexed Armenia, all of the area of what was once Assyria and then the southern portion, the old Sumer, and advancing as far south as the Persian Gulf. It was a notable campaign, but it was not appreciated by the Persians, who attacked his rear as he was hastening to take care of a revolt by the Jews. He died on the way home, in Cilicia, in 117 A.D. His successor, Hadrian, decided to abandon Trajan's eastern conquests and allowed the Persians to regain control over Mesopotamia; his only war of consequence, and a minor one at that for the Romans, was the suppression of a great Jewish revolt in 132 A.D. The resistance of the Jews against superior, better-armed, and more experienced Roman troops was heroic, but Hadrian laid waste the entire country in putting down the rebels in three years of warfare. After that the Jews were forbidden to visit Jerusalem, which the Romans renamed Aelia Capitolina.

Hadrian set the Romans' eastern boundary on the Euphrates. Again little is known of the events beyond the river in the following century. Christianity began to gain converts in the area, where the faith was not illegal as it was under the Romans. The main source of information about the situation east of the Euphrates comes from Christian sources. The Romans could not let Mesopotamia alone, however, and made repeated incursions over the Euphrates, either crossing the river and the steppelands on foot and horse, or attacking through the Mesopotamian delta by boat. Peace and war alternated, and when the Romans could not maintain their rule through puppet kings and governors subservient to their wills, the Arsacids returned.

We have not seen the end of Iranian adventurer nomad kings. Early in the third century the Arsacids had lost control of their empire up to the Tigris, and consolidated their strength behind the river's eastern banks. In 226 A.D. a new group of Iranians, the Sassanids (named after a magus, a Zoroastrian priest, called Sassan) overthrew the Parthian Arsacids and initiated a widespread political and religious reform. Their barbaric energies presented a real challenge to Roman strength, now weakening as the result of ceaseless turmoil in that empire. Zoroastrianism underwent a purification. The Hellenizing tendencies, which under the Arsacids had brought to the fore various deities foreign to the early monotheism of Ahura Mazda, were pushed to the background. Zoroastrianism—specifically the worship of the Supreme God Ahura Mazda— which had existed as the favored cultus of the Persians, became the empire's official religion.

A gnarled, cheerful monk of the ancient Chaldean Nestorian church stands before his monastery. The church is based on the teachings of Nestorius, bishop of Constantinople (428–431)

Toward the middle of the third century the great Sassanian king Shapur I, noted as a soldier and empire-builder of wide interests and high intelligence, swept across Mesopotamia and into Syria, winning victories in which the Romans were savagely and cruelly destroyed. In a few short years Shapur had conquered three Roman emperors: Gordian III, Philip the Arab, and Valarian, the latter conquest an event that was proudly commemorated in rock carvings at the great funerary complex of the Iranians at Naqsh-i-Ustam. The Romans, weakened severely, withdrew from further conflict; several of their generals were assassinated, and it looked as if Roman power had finally waned. But the great empire was not easily forgotten. Renewing their energies with new emperors and new generals, the Romans returned again and again to challenge the Sassanids. Treaties were signed and broken, puppets installed and removed. But the empire, beset by barbarian tribes in Europe and social unrest at home, was in a precarious condition.

In 312 and 313 the struggle took a religious turn. The young general Constantine seized the throne after a series of civil wars with other claimants. Though a pagan he had a religious dream the night before his last and greatest battle, in which he heard the command to conquer in the sign of Christ, the XP (or *chi rho*). With his victory Constantine granted tolerance to Christians, hitherto proscribed, and confirmed his act the next year with the Edict of Milan. In 324 he founded a new capital on the site of an ancient Greek town, Byzantion, on the Hellespont facing Asia Minor. The city was named after the emperor, Constantinople, and the empire was known as Byzantium. The new "Rome"—the people were still known as Romans, and the term *Rum* lasted for another 1,100 years—was soon involved in a series of religious squabbles among the Christians involving the nature of Christ. The disputes may seem remote to the present age, but they brought civil wars, the loss of entire sections of the empire, wars between lands following different interpretations, and helped prepare the ground for the acceptance of Islam centuries later. There were many variations on the basic theme, and I can give here only the two major views divergent from the one that came to be accepted as the orthodox one. Briefly, the majority of the bishops and the faithful believed that Jesus was the Son of God the Father, and was both God and man. An Alexandrian priest named Arius, however, said—roughly summarized—that if the Son is begotten of the Father, there was then a time when the Son did not exist: Therefore the Son is not from eternity and is not God. In 325 Constantine, though not a Christian, called a meeting at Nicea, across the straits from the capital, to discuss the controversy. The Egyptian bishops, who tended to follow Arius, after much acrimony mostly submitted to the will of the majority, but Arianism continued, complicated by arguments among the Arians themselves over other points. A second major dispute broke out in the next century over a doctrine called Nestorianism, after a Syrian-born patriarch Nestorius. In contrast to the orthodox belief that there was but one Person in Christ, at once God and man, Nestorius taught that the two aspects were separate, one divine, the other human. Though Nestorius was anathematized, his views were popular in the East, especially in Mesopotamia and Persia, where they blended with certain aspects of Zoroastrianism.

Constantine's acceptance of Christianity, which soon became the official religion of the Roman empire, now put Mesopotamian and Iranian Christians in a new light. The Sassanids could see them as nothing but subversive, holding allegiance not to the Persian emperor but to the Roman. In 350 persecutions of Christians began.

So the days, the years, and centuries slid by, king against
king, empire against empire, the subjects shifting from orthodoxy to heresy, from Christianity to Zoroastrianism and back,
or perhaps to some other faith, like that of Mani. Mani, a
Persian who visited India and was impressed by the Buddhist
Middle Way, added Buddhism to both of the other religions,
and spread his doctrine, called Manichaeism, all over both
empires, causing endless trouble for the orthodox on either
side. The rivers flooded and dried up, shifted and straightened;
cities founded and declined. There were famines, drought,
barbarians, palace revolts, and persecution of the righteous as
well as of the evil. It could not have been a period of much enjoyment for the average man, and historians tend to gloss over
it. Syria, Mesopotamia, and Iran were in constant turmoil,
to say nothing of the Romans' dual empire, its stronger half in
the East, its weaker still hanging on in Rome, now a city declining into a large village, its streets weedy and grass-grown
and serving as pastures for cattle.

Mention must be made of one more explosion. In 602 Phocas
became emperor of Byzantium. He attempted to clean up the
Sassanids forever, to get them off the Romans' eastern frontier.
A final victory came in 608, not for Phocas but for the Sassanian king Khosrau II. He dealt the Romans a decisive blow,
though many of their garrisons fought bravely and to the
death. Khosrau not only pushed the Romans out of Mesopotamia but captured many of their other long-held provinces.
Further, he deported large numbers of the troublesome orthodox Christians to his easternmost lands. Khosrau's grand-
father, Khosrau I the Blessed, had been noted for the
benevolence of his rule, having introduced a series of reforms,
lessened the burden of taxes, and promoted the arts, sciences,
and literature. But Khosrau II was a different man. Cruel and

grasping, he crushed the people under his taxes, personally amassing enormous sums of money and ravishing the western areas of Asia Minor with his armies, conquering Damascus and Jerusalem, where he stole the esteemed and honored relic so sacred to Christianity, the True Cross found by Constantine's mother, Saint Helena, in the fourth century. Khosrau was murdered by his own son, Kavad II, who in his six short months of rule managed to lose both Mesopotamia and the True Cross to the Romans, who restored it to Jerusalem. The Arian and Nestorian Christians of Mesopotamia, suffering under Zoroastrianism, found that rule by an unsympathetic ecclesiastical orthodoxy, which the Romans allowed to take over, was even worse.

But soon Roman-Persian, Zoroastrian-Christian-heretical conflicts would become irrelevant, for the new force of Islam would wipe away everything in one vast sweep. When the Muslims appeared out of the Arabian desert so close to Mesopotamia, the last Sassanian emperor, Yazdakart III, one of but twelve kings in the twelve years after Khosrau II, could barely assemble an army to meet the enemy. He was hardly the man for the throne. The Sassanian empire had already disintegrated into several petty states and was incapable of resisting any foe. But the die-hard ministers of the court, determined for a show of legitimacy, installed Yazdakart as king after finding this scion of Khosrau II hiding in a cave in Persia. With much trepidation the king crossed the Tigris and the Euphrates to meet the Arabs on the desert plain at al-Qadisiyyah in 637 and was soundly defeated. Like Darius so many centuries earlier, Yazdakart turned and fled, to Merv near Afghanistan, where, like Darius, he was finally assassinated.

8

THE ARAB
CONQUEST

MOST OF THE ARABIAN PENINSULA IS NOT FIT, FROM WANT OF
moisture, for producing grain; what grains the Arabs used in
the past came from Persia. In Muhammad's time the Arabs
lived by the breeding of camels, horses, and sheep. The worth
of all things was estimated in camels, the common currency in
business transactions. The horse was a luxury, not a necessity,
and as vulnerable as man in the heat of the waterless desert.
Date palms were grown, then as now, in spots watered by
permanent wells. Irrigation was practiced by means of the
Persian wheel, a simple arrangement of revolving scoops or
buckets turned by a camel. The peninsula does not contain any
permanent stream nor any fountain of waters which are not
soon swallowed up by the sand. Rains, brought by the southwest monsoon from the Indian Ocean, fall upon the lofty
mountain ranges of al-Yemen in the south during the summer
months. The rest of the Arabian highlands, which are not ex-

tensive, are visited only by showers during the months of winter and spring; they bring a rapid growth of the long dormant herbage and grasses over the great wastes of central Arabia and the replenishing of many watering places which, during the hot seasons, are dry. The settlements of the tribes are around traditional water holes which do not fail in the summer. As soon as the great upland downs of Nejd become covered with the young pasture, the tribesmen move forth with their herds and occupy their spring quarters until the fierce heat and drought of the vernal—spring—equinox forces them back to their wells. This pleasant season of grass and flowers and of abundance brings out the peninsula's fauna as well: wild ox, white antelope, wild asses, wolves, foxes, hyenas, eagles, vultures, ostriches, hawks, and sandgrouse. The lion is rare, and for hunting the Arab sportsman was likely to go to the reedy swamps along the lower Euphrates.

It was and is a society as savage as the land.

Laws of wild justice, of the blood feud, are celebrated in the early, pre-Muslim poetry, and the proscriptions of the Prophet could not stop the taking of lives.

> He who does not keep his foe away from his wells
>   with sword and spear
>   is broken and spoiled;
> He who does not use roughness
>   him shall men wrong.

Other lines speak of the blood feud:

> Hearts are cured of sickness
> whether men war against us
> or we carry death among them.
>   Dying, slaying,
>   healing comes.

A fierce world. Blood sacrifices. At the Ka'ba at Mecca, a pagan shrine before the Prophet announced its sanctity to Allah the Supreme, camels, sheep, and goats were offered. The sixth-century Byzantine historian, Procopius of Caesaria, recorded that an Arab prince named al-Mundhir offered up the son of his rival al-Harith to the goddess al-Uzza. He also is said to have put to death as a sacrifice to al-Uzza four hundred captive "nuns" or temple women.

The Arabs, divided into tribes and clans, were noted by other peoples as being fearless, fierce, sensual, keen-witted, and materialistic, born traders and marauders. The state of Arab society when the Prophet was born is "imperfectly known," cautiously notes one recent historian.

Muhammad was born in 570 A.D. in Mecca, a small, prosperous city subsisting on the caravan route which ran north and south. Even before his birth Mecca was a sacred city, with a pagan sanctuary, the Ka'ba, a huge cube of stone said to have been built by the Prophet Abraham upon a heavenly model. A yearly festival, the hajj, or pilgrimage, was celebrated even then; later it became one of the five duties of the devout Muslim. Muhammad's tribe was the Quiraish, which held certain valuable concessions dealing with the pilgrim trade in the city. After a youth of some poverty, tending herds for relatives, he entered the employ of a wealthy widow named Kadijah and made a caravan trip on her behalf to Syria, about 594. Though she was twenty years older, Muhammad married her, and from then on took charge of her business affairs, a responsibility he executed with success. But he was at heart a mystic rather than a businessman. About the age of forty he began to have religious experiences of an unusual sort, beginning with one in which he saw the Angel Gabriel. Muhammad had retired to a cave outside Mecca to spend the night in meditation.

Here Gabriel appeared and uttered the famous words, "Recite! recite! in the name of the Lord!" thus giving the world the opening phrase of the Qur'an, the most sacred book of Islam.

The visitations from the angel continued, and through them, first at Mecca and then at Yathrib (later called Medina), Muhammad received the entire Qur'an, though in no special order. What Gabriel told him, Muhammad dictated to his closest followers, the texts being collated after his death. In the beginning Muhammad made few converts to the message he was receiving, that of the Uniqueness and Oneness of Allah, God, and of man's total submission to Him. (Islam, the faith Muhammad preached, means "submission," and Muslim means "one who submits.") But after many vicissitudes, including a forced flight to Yathrib and a victorious return with an army of followers to Mecca, which now submitted to him, the Prophet was able to established the primacy and correctness of Islam for the Arabs of the scattered and often warring tribes of the peninsula.

What Muhammad taught is of the essence for the next events in Mesopotamia, now entering virtual chaos under the decline of the last of the Sassanids.

Muhammad considered himself—and this was taught in the Qur'an as received from Gabriel—as the last and the greatest of the prophets—messengers commisisoned by the One God to teach the true monotheistic faith, following the line of the Hebrew prophets such as Noah, Abraham, Moses, and even including Jesus and John the Baptist. The faith of the "people of the Book," as he called both the Jews and the Christians, had been corrupted by the sins of both, and now it was the privilege and responsibility of the Muslims to proclaim the faith renewed and purified. Muslim theology and philosophy grew to complex proportions in later centuries, but the basic doctrines, the core beliefs of Islam, could be summarized in these basic points:

The one transcendent God (Allah), Creator of all else, merciful and just.

The moral law He laid down for all mankind forever.

The coming Judgment, which would end in either Hell or Paradise, conceived in both spiritual and materialistic terms, the form of the latter being expressed in the quintessence of all the pains or the pleasures of the senses of this life.

Muhammad's proclamation of Islam transcended the old, strict, narrow adherence of the Arabs to tribe, clan, and family. Now *all* mankind, Arab and non-Arab, black and brown as well as white, would be included in the divine plan. It was the responsibility of each individual to work out his own salvation within the framework of the plan. So to traditional Arab tribal notions of honor and justice Muhammad added a moral law applicable to all mankind.

All but a few of the tribes of the Arabian peninsula quickly accepted Islam; Muhammad quickly overcame a few recalcitrant Bedouin tribes by force. Arabia could thus be considered totally and safely Muslim, and Muhammad was now not only the Prophet of the "restored" religion but the ruler of a rather large area containing a cohesive people—the Arab tribes united not only by language and custom but welded into an effective, aggressive force psychologically, militarily, and religiously. He was to be considered the supreme leader of an army of tremendous strength and motivation. He now began a Holy War against the Byzantine areas of Syria, but lost the first battle. After that he was to gain one victory after another, his Muslim Arabs overrunning small settlements of Jews and Christians in northwest Arabia and western Mesopotamia. These victories confirmed his belief that he was the divinely appointed Messenger of Allah and that his mission was the conversion of the world to Islam. In June, 632 A.D., while preparing a major expedition against the Byzantines, Muhammad died.

The new power of Islam, religious as well as secular, might have disintegrated without such a powerful and charismatic leader as Muhammad, but it had gained enough momentum that his closest associates, known as the Companions, his inner circle, and their generals could sweep through the Fertile Crescent scoring one victory after another.

Even as Muhammad lay unburied the Companions chose one of their number, the Prophet's uncle Abu Bakr, as khalif, or deputy. The office of khalif, for a few centuries the most important in Islam, engendered disputes of continent-shaking magnitude. Less than thirty years after Muhammad's death one of these disputes resulted in a major split in the Muslims, forming two groups, the Sunnis, the more "orthodox" (because they followed the sunna, the accepted practice and beliefs of the larger portion of the Islamic community) and the Shi'a, who followed Muhammad's son-in-law Ali, the fourth khalif. The Shi'a, more mystical and emotional than the Sunni, soon broke into a number of sub-groups, many influenced by millennial doctrines among the Christians and especially the Zoroastrians.

Abu Bakr, an old man, died after two years as khalif. As he lay in his final illness, he appointed Umar ibn al-Khattab, one of the Companions, as the next khalif. Under Umar's khalifate Syria, Palestine, Armenia, and Egypt were invaded and successfully incorporated into the new Muslim empire. One of Umar's generals invaded Mesopotamia, which the Arabs called

 The Umayyads took over the old basilica of St. John the Baptist and turned it into a mosque, which it is still today. The Great Mosque is one of the leading religious centers of Damascus. The saint's head is still venerated at the mosque.

Iraq, and in a decisive battle at al-Qadisiyyah in 637, destroyed
the main power of the Sassanid army and opened the way to
an invasion of Persia. Four years later all of Persia was in Arab
hands, and the remnants of the Sassanids pushed off the historical scene. In large numbers the people of the newly conquered lands, from west to east, joined Islam. The transition
from Christianity, whether orthodox or heretical, and from
Zoroastrianism, could not have been traumatic for many of
the converts. The Oneness of Allah was a doctrine easily acceptable to people whose faith was based on broad beliefs and
not on deep theological grounds, especially to Christians like
the Arians, who did not accept Christ as coequal with the
Father, nor the Nestorians, with their troublesome views of
the divinity of Jesus, nor of various others that held equally
unorthodox doctrines. And many Zoroastrians could see that
Allah and Ahura Mazda were undoubtedly the same Supreme
Lord. The legend of conversion to Islam by the sword is but
partly true. The peoples of North Africa, Syria, Palestine,
Mesopotamia, and Persia had but minor adjustments to make
to accept Muhammad as the last of the prophets, successor to
Abraham, Moses, Jesus, and even Zoroaster.

Umar was a stern ruler but a just one. He would walk the
streets of the cities at night in disguise, looking for orphans or
the destitute to help; he wore a patched robe in the kind of
saintly poverty that was an ideal preached by the Prophet
Muhammad. He was also an energetic city-builder, founding
the two important cities of Kufa on the Euphrates and Basra
on the confluence of both the Mesopotamian rivers. After ten
years as khalif Umar was assassinated by a Persian slave with a
poisoned dagger as he prayed in the mosque at Medina.

The next khalif, Uthman ibn Affran, like his predecessors,
was a Companion and a saintly man. He was nominated to the

khalifate by the Companions themselves. Unfortunately he was not an administrator or a ruler, and he fell under the influence of his clan, which apportioned the valuable governing and civil posts among themselves, ousting Umar's more wisely selected men. The new governors, who had been among the men who opposed Muhammad until the end, taxed heavily and oppressed their people, Arab and non-Arab alike. Protests began, mainly in Egypt and Iraq, and soon the turmoil was out of hand. Uthman was killed in 656 by Muslim rebels while reading the Qur'an at home.

The fourth khalif seemed like a logical choice. He was Ali ibn Abu Talib, not only a Companion but Muhammad's cousin and son-in-law, and the second or third person known to embrace Islam. His good qualities were unparalleled; he was noted for his honesty, integrity, piety, modesty, wisdom, wide knowledge, and as a forceful speaker and great warrior, perhaps one of Islam's best. In short the perfect Muslim. Unfortunately he became the focal point of clan and family rivalries arising out of the social turmoil he had inherited from Uthman. Rebels were actively campaigning against the khalifate, and Ali had to take to the field in an attempt to suppress them. His khalifate, which lasted only five years, survived under tragic circumstances, marked by continual bloodshed and treachery on the part of enemies and even friends. Uthman's relatives accused Ali, who was innocent, of defending the murderers, and civil war ensued, the blood feuds lasting for generations. In a pitched battle with Uthman's cousin Mu'awiyah, when Ali was on the point of victory, his opponent called for a judgment to be made not by arms but by resorting to the Qur'an, each of the two contestants to appoint one man as representative. Ali's man, speaking first, said the only solution was for both Ali and Mu'awiyah to withdraw and for someone else to become khalif, thus ending the warring. But Mu'awiyah's representative said that since Ali had now withdrawn as khalif, the only person who could be khalif was Mu'awiyah.

Ali now prepared for a second war against Mu'awiyah, but before he could take on his enemy, a group of his own followers denounced him for accepting a man-made judgment, thus betraying his faith; moreover this group, known as the Khawarij, or Seceders, also denounced Uthman and Mu'awiyah as unbelievers. In July, 659, Ali overcame the Khawarij in a massive battle in which it is said 40,000 lives were lost, but before he could turn to his other opponent, he was assassinated by a Khawarij partisan as he entered the mosque at Kufa, which he had made his capital. Properly, Ali's son al-Hasan should then have been khalif, but he decided that enough bloodshed had occurred already (he was murdered later), and he relinquished the khalifate to Mu'awiyah, who moved the center of religious and secular rule to Damascus.

The dynasty of khalifates he founded was known as the Umayyads, after his tribal name, and ruled from 661 to 750, fourteen khalifates being numbered in that time. We move quickly through this period. The Umayyads were known as capable but harsh rulers, quick to tax and quick to war. Though they represented the orthodox khalifate, they were generally considered to be usurpers, and Ali, martyred, and his sons, also martyred in the cause, came to be popular points of both resistance and devotion. Murders—of khalifs or opponents—were constant during Umayyad reign, and the movement that coalesced around the memory of the martyrs, the Shi'a, caused a constant state of civil war.

Shi'ism, though Muslim in content and descending from the Prophet himself, shows an even more intense devotion to the tragic house of Ali and his sons Hasan and Husayn, whose festivals are celebrated yearly with much pageantry, emotion, and mystical release, especially in eastern Iraq, Iran, and parts of Pakistan and India—those areas which had once been Zoroastrian and had an overlay of Islamic doctrines superimposed upon an underlying core of Zoroastrianism. Many Zoroastrian themes were and are to be found in the Shi'a forms of Islam, notably the concept of the Hidden Imam, or leader, an idea based on the Zoroastrian belief that one of their Prophet's disciples, Prince Peshotan, has been waiting in a cave to return someday to save the world. Some forms of Shi'ism, such as the Seveners and the Twelvers, believe in a series of semidivine leaders, the Imams, the last of which is yet to come. Even the Christian belief in the Second Coming of Jesus at the Apocalypse may have reappeared in Shi'a form.

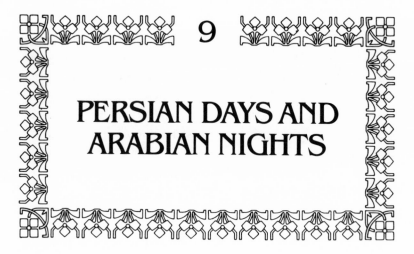

9

PERSIAN DAYS AND ARABIAN NIGHTS

THE ARABS LIKED THE FERTILE CRESCENT BECAUSE OF ITS LUSH lands and running waters. The Umayyads had chosen Damascus as their capital, but their successors preferred Iraq, for (in the words of one of their historians) it was "the center of this world, the navel of the earth," with regular climate and seasons. "The weather is temperate, the soil is rich, the water is sweet, the trees are thriving, the fruit luscious, the seeds are fertile, good things are abundant, and springs are easily found." Another historian remarked, "The most elegant country is Iraq. It is the one which most enlightens the heart and sharpens the mind and in which the soul is most at ease and thought is most refined, if means suffice."

Mu'awiya had founded his khalifate in Damascus because it was far from the feuding of Mecca and Medina, and the succeeding Umayyads had kept it there because they had grown up in the city and found their greatest support in it. Outside

Syria the Umayyads were unpopular and were accused of impiety and of worldy ambitions. Uprisings against them broke out regularly, particularly in Hejaz in the north of the Arabian peninsula, and in Iraq. But within their limits, imposed by the hostility of their secular and religious foes, they developed the administration of their area well, established a mail service to the far-flung parts of the Muslim empire, replaced Greek and Latin with Arabic as the common language, and embarked upon a building program which resulted in many magnificent mosques and palaces. Their armies reached as far as Spain in the west, and the Sind and the Punjab, both Indian provinces, and the Turkestan desert in the east. Also they were able, from time to time, to threaten the Byzantine capital, Constaninople. But their enemies increased, and in addition to the various branches of the Shi'a, another formidable rival, the Abbasids, appeared, named after Muhammad's paternal uncle, al-Abbas, which gave them much authority over other tribes. All over Arabia and Iraq, and as far as Persia, the Muslims were preparing to attack the Umayyads. One of the leaders of the growing rebellion was an Arab named al-Mansur.

One day a group of people gathered in the presence of al-Mansur, and they spoke of the Umayyad Khalifs, their way of life, their conduct of affairs, and the cause which led to their loss of power. Al-Mansur said, "Abd al-Malik was a tyrant who never thought of what he said, Sulayman cared only for his belly and his private parts. Umar ibn al-Aziz [the only khalif the Abbasids respected] was a one-eyed man among the blind. . . . The Umayyads had the highest things from God, but their authority passed to their pampered sons, whose only care was the pursuit of passion and the quest for pleasure in these things which are forbidden by Almighty God, unaware of God's stealthy retribution and lulled by His cunning . . . God deprived them of power, covered them with shame, and withdrew His grace from them."

Retribution struck first at Khurasan, formerly known as Elam; here the Umayyad governor was attacked and defeated by rebels; the khalif at Damascus, engaged with his own rebellious tribes, could not send any aid. Now the rebels, the Abbasids, took control of Iraq, capturing Kufa in 749. The final battle took place on the Syrian-Iraqi border in April, 750. Here the rebel Abu al-Abbas ibn Muhammad ibn Ali ibn Abd Allah ibn al-Abbas (his extensive name gives his pedigree back to Muhammad's uncle) defeated the last Umayyad khalif, Marwan ibn Muhammad, who fled to Egypt after losing his army, only to be found in his hiding place and murdered. But a year before the battle al-Abbas, more commonly known as al-Saffah, the Bloodthirsty, had himself proclaimed khalif at the mosque at Kufa, and received the homage of the people.

No one mourned Marwan. He had been equally bloodthirsty, having assassinated his cousin, the Crown Prince Amir ibn Sa'id, during a private audience. The prince's head was thrown outside the palace to his supporters, who were waiting for him, along with some gold pieces. Not only was the last Umayyad khalif done away with, but so were the traces and remains of his predecessors, their tombs being opened under al-Saffah's orders and their dust and bones scattered about. The remaining living Umayyads were murdered. Al-Saffah lived four years, denouncing the extravagances and impieties of the Umayyads, and proclaiming a life of true Islamic austerity for himself and the faithful. He died a natural death. He was succeeded by Abu Ja'far, known as al-Mansur, Rendered

 Damascus, here seen from the air, is one of the most beautiful cities of the world. It had been the capital of the Umayyad dynasty until the Abbasids rebelled and moved the seat of power to Iraq, in the heart of Mesopotamia. The large rectangular building seen in the picture is the Great Mosque.

Victorious by God, just as bloodthirsty but perhaps more interesting.

Many of the Abbasid generals had been non-Arabs. The Abbasids, unlike the Umayyads, had no prejudice against non-Arabs and took them into their khalifate. But in a sweep of potentially dangerous "foreigners" al-Mansur eliminated some of the non-Arabs who had been most responsible for destroying the Umayyads. He invited his chief general, Abu Muslim al-Khurasani (a Persian by his name) to an audience. In a familiar scene the general's staff was waiting outside the gates of the palace, expecting that their chief would receive some singular honor. His head was thrown to them from the palace steps. Other potential enemies were also eliminated.

Yet the general policy of the Abbasids was far more open than that of the Umayyads. The Abbasids made full use of the Persian administrative system they had inherited, and worked with what existed in other areas, rather than attempting to place Arab kinsmen in important and sensitive posts. The races they ruled were many: not only Arabs but Byzantines, Turks, Jews, Indians, blacks, and all the mixed peoples of Mesopotamia. Non-Arab wives became the rule rather than the exception; because of the close ties to Iran many of the wives were Persian, which had a profound effect on the attitudes and the development of the khalifate. Persian become the second language of Islam, following Arabic, and the heritage of all cultures touched upon by Islam was drawn into its orbit, especially Greek, which resulted in the translation of many of the classical authors and philosophers; on the other side of the empire, much learning from India was taken up by Arab scholars.

The first Abbasid khalifs emphasized their religious spartanism. They adopted simple clothing; on ceremonial occasions they wore a cloak which they claimed had been the Prophet's own. But they soon fell into the same lascivious, luxury-loving, cruel ways of life that they had so condemned among the Umayyads. Their laws, imposed at whim, were harshly devised and harshly executed. They adopted the frightening institution of the *nil*, a piece of leather spread before the throne of the khalif, on which he could watch his enemies beheaded by his executioner, who always stood ready beside him.

The Abbasids' rule had many weaknesses, chief of which was a lessening of the heroic virtues the Arabs had enjoyed in the peninsula. In Mesopotamia—Iraq—after initially condemning the Umayyads for their servile enjoyment of luxury and sensuality, the Abbasids themselves soon relapsed, and even during the first century lost control of the khalifate, which was taken over by the wazirs (or viziers), the chief ministers, who ruled through the figureheads of the khalifs.

The wazirs were most often Persians. In general the Persians, with their long history, their traditions and civilization, were more cultured than the unsophisticated Arabs, only recently removed from the desert. They had been treated harshly by the Umayyads, but under the Abbasids their intellectual qualities and administrative genius were well regarded and rewarded. Partly because of the Umayyad hostility to all things Persian, the Persians had favored Shi'ism, and they had taken the attitude of *taqiyah*, which means the virtue of hiding one's true loyalty for safety. But the Persians' Shi'ism was more than a reaction to the Umayyads. Under the veneer of Islam certain Persians retained their original Zoroastrianism, or converted it into a form of Islam known as Sufism, a mystical way which was often anathema to the more orthodox Sunnis.

The Umayyad khalif Umar ibn al-Azziz, noted for his ex-

treme rectitude and piety, had also been extreme in dealing
with the Zoroastrians, forcing conversions to Islam and burning the faith's sacred texts. Many Zoroastrians fled rather than
submit, going either to China or India; only the latter, the
Parsis, have survived. The "converts" began to influence Islam
through its Shi'ite form, so that even today Persian Muslims are
not regarded as fully orthodox by the more rigid Sunni. Moreover Islam among the Persians and many Iraqis took the mystical form of Sufism, founding esoteric brotherhoods and lodges,
and using code phrases acceptable to Muslims but with Zoroastrian meanings. To note some of the more obvious and
easily understood terms: the Zoroastrian prayer hall, presided
over by a Persian priest, became the tavern; sacred spiritual
teaching was the wine; divine ecstasy was intoxication, the
teacher the wine-bearer. Erotic terms in their poetry portrayed
Allah as the Beloved, and union with the Beloved was absorp-
tion in Ahura Mazda. The bird in the cage—a familiar Sufi
phrase—was the longing of the soul for release from the
bonds of the mundane into the universal source of Divine
Wisdom.

Al Saffah had begun his khalifate at Kufa but then had moved
it to a town called Hashimiyya, after the Meccan tribe from
which the Abbasids were descended. After he died (in 754
A.D.) his son al-Mansur founded another city, which he gave
the same name. But three years later, while on a warring expedition, he crossed the Tigris and found a small village called
Baghdad on a most favorable site.

"What is the name of this place?"
"Baghdad," they answered.
"By God," said the khalif, "this is indeed the city which

my father told me I must build, in which I must live, and in which my descendants after me will live. Kings were unaware of it before and since Islam until God's plans for me and orders to me are accomplished. . . . Praise be to God who preserved it for me and caused all those who came before me to neglect it. By God, I shall build it. Then I shall dwell in it as long as I live, and my descendants shall dwell in it after me. It will surely be the most flourishing city in the world. Then I shall found four other cities, none of which shall ever be ruined.

Al-Mansur did found the other four (Rafiqa, Malatya, Missis, and Mansura, the latter in India, none well known), but it was Baghdad that was to be famous for all time. Al-Mansur had seen that it would be a center of trade, for it lay at the point where the Tigris and the Euphrates were closest to each other and attainable by ship from the Persian Gulf, as well as by ships coming downstream from Mosul. It also lay on a convenient east-west trade route between Persia and Syria and Egypt.

In 758 al-Mansur laid out the plan for the new city, laying the foundations at a moment chosen as propitious by his astronomers. What was of unusual interest was its shape: He made of it a round city, the only round city known then in the whole world. It had four gates. Its diameter was 5,000 black cubits, such a cubit measuring about eighteen inches. Thus it was almost a mile and a half in diameter. Even before construction started he called together 100,000 workmen—architects, engineers, masons, laborers, craftsmen, carpenters, smiths, and diggers.

The palace was placed in the center of a great square, in the center of the circle. Adjoining the palace was the cathedral mosque; there were no other buildings except for two for the

 This is a Bedouin with his camels in the Arabian desert. The government has built houses for the nomadic tribes, but the men prefer to live in tents as in the past, while they keep the women in the new permanent homes.

police and the palace horse guards. Around the square were the dwellings of the khalif's sons, the quarters of the black slaves, the treasury, the arsenal, the chancery, the office of the land tax, public kitchens, and various government offices. The remainder of the city was turned over, in quarters, to various officials, to traders and businessmen, and ordinary people. Avenues were laid out fifty cubits wide, with streets of sixteen cubits, and dead-end alleys as needed.

And this was the city of the Arabian Nights.

For centuries Baghdad was the center of civilization. Not only was the wealth of the world concentrated there, but so was its intellect. Rome, once the capital of half a million people, had declined into a weedy town of 50,000 peasants, in whose empty streets cattle browsed. London and Paris were but villages, and Constantinople, the Byzantine capital, but a second-rate city, for it was to Baghdad that everyone came. In the only other empire of any size and power, the Holy Roman Empire founded by Charlemagne, the nobles could barely write their names, and nothing else; under the Abbasids everyone was expected to be educated. The universities of Baghdad and Nippur were founded centuries before the famous institutions of Paris, Bologna, and Salerno; at the far end of the Arab world, at Cordova in Spain, the first free schools in the Western world were opened under Muslim auspices. The classical Greeks—Aristotle, Plato, Euclid, Archimedes, Hippocrates— were translated into Arabic (and later retranslated into Latin and the Western languages). From the East, too, there were important contributions. One day a wandering Indian scholar, looking for a patron (he had, of course, come to the right place), appeared at al-Mansur's court with two manuscripts under his arm, one dealing with astronomy, the other with mathematics. Al-Mansur ordered them translated into Arabic. The book about astronomy served as the model for Arab studies and experiments, and laid the basis for the scientific understanding of the cosmos. Knowledge of the stars was important for the Arabs, for in the trackless desert and at sea, the stars' positions could guide people traveling at night. Also the astrologers believed that the heavenly bodies were influential in all human affairs and could give information about terrestrial happenings. Moreover there was a far more practical reason for correct astronomical charts: With them a Muslim could always find the true direction of the Ka'ba at Mecca, toward which all prayer had to be directed no matter where one was—north, east, south, or west.

The Indian treatise about mathematics was even more important, for it was needed for an understanding of astronomy and, with few exceptions, for virtually all other subjects. The pre-Islamic Arabs were said not to be able to count over a thousand, and what they inherited in Mesopotamia and Persia was an incomplete system, for the duodecimal system (counting on a basis of twelve, or even sixty) was common. Virtually all people west of India—the Babylonians, Greeks, Romans, Arabs, and so on—used letters as numerals, while the Indians had developed separate characters for each number. Also they had made an important discovery, the concept of the point, or zero, the void, which made it possible to count in ordered series less than one, and enabled the mathematician (or the businessman) to "keep the rows," as the Arabs expressed it, that is, to maintain each figure in its place in the series of powers. The Arabs called the Indian numerals "Hindi," while we know them as "Arabic numerals."

One of the borrowings from India was the charming form of literature known as the fable. Al-Muqaffa, a Persian converted from Zoroastrianism, adapted some ancient Indian stories from a work called the *Panchtantra*, in which animals are personified and have experiences which are related to serve a moral point. Al-Muqaffa's stories were purportedly told by an Indian brahmin called Bidpai. So facile in language and elegant in style was the Arabic translation that it became a classic in Arabic literature, and was retranslated into forty other languages from Indonesia to Iceland. Perhaps the unlucky al-Muqaffa had a foreboding of his end when he wrote such stories as "The Ox and the Lion," or even more so "The Raven, the Wolf, the Fox, the Lion, and the Camel," which depicts the sad death of the ox and the camel. For al-Mansur suspected that al-Muqaffa had both secret—subversive—Zoroastrian and political intentions, and he ordered the hapless author drawn and quartered and cast into a bakeoven.

A more famous work, also with Indian ancestry, is the world-known *Arabian Nights*, or more properly, *Thousand and One Nights* (in Arabic, *Alf Layla wa-Layla*), a collection of short stories, romances, fables, parables, fairy tales, and legends. The various pieces are set in Baghdad, Egypt, Persia, and other parts of the khalifate and abroad, and are based upon a common device, a narrator entertaining a group of people. In this case the narrator is the young Scheherazade, who tells stories to the Persian king Shahryar. She had a good reason for the stories, for the king, after finding his wife unfaithful, had put her to death, and since then had taken a new wife every day and executed her the following morning. Eventually Shahryar ran out of candidates (they could not have been willing ones, anyway). Scheherazade, one of the wazir's daughters, wanted to be queen, but a live one. She persuaded her father to give her in marriage to the king, having worked out a scheme for avoiding execution. Each night she began a story but did not finish it, promising to complete it the next day if the king did not kill her. And so she survived until the shah ultimately abandoned his cruel plan.

The core of the work, apparently of Indian origin, was un-doubtedly transmitted orally, but written versions appeared about the end of the seventh century A.D., with continual additions after that, including material from all over the khalifate and abroad; some stories come from the time of the wars against the Crusaders, and others were brought to the Middle East by the Turks and Mongols in later centuries. Because of the mixed origins of the stories the Arabic is often poor and ungrammatical. But the individual pieces include an immense variety, few of which have ever appeared in Western versions. Still we know about Sinbad the Sailor, Ali Baba and the Forty Thieves, Aladdin and the Magic Lamp, and the Merchant and the Djinns. The Western translations have been poorly done or highly expurgated, for, as one expert wrote, "certain stories are not for juvenile reading." The translations by John Payne and Richard Burton are the best and are complete, but they are done in an archaic form of English, which makes reading difficult; Burton's has excellent commentaries and notes, for Burton knew Arabic and Arab ways as well as any Arab.

The city grew and matured rapidly. Thirty-two years after the death of al-Saffah, the Bloodshedder, the first Abbasid khalif, Baghdad reached the full glory and opulence of the Arabian Nights under the famous Harun al-Rashid, the fifth of the dynasty, who ruled for the unusually long period 786 to 809. It was Harun who established the atmosphere of sensuality, luxury, and cruelty we associate with this period. He was not an especially great nor even good ruler, though he and his court were famous as far away as Aachen, where the

Frankish emperor Charlemagne ruled; Harun and Charlemagne exchanged gifts upon occasion, and may even have had diplomatic relations. The hypnotic effect of Harun's court, Persian and not desert-Arab in its spirit, ran from one end of the empire to the other, instilling even the simplest with the fatal love of luxury, the lasciviousness which had faulted the Umayyads in the eyes of the Abbasid rebels.

Fortunes equivalent to the greatest today were made in Baghdad and elsewhere in Iraq and Persia. The Persian Barmaki family, a renowned house which furnished wazirs of the most illustrious kind under Mansur and his successors, reached such power and wealth that Harun decided to liquidate them. Aside from the family's various palaces, villages and estates, the fortune was said to have been worth over $30,000,000. Harun's brother, a professional singer, received over $2,000,000 in gifts from the khalif alone. All the male members of the Hashimite clan of the Quraysh, Muhammad's own family, to which the Abbasids belonged, received regular and large pensions from the state treasury merely because of their origin. One of Harun's wives, Zubaydah, beautiful and talented according to the accounts, and an Arab, unlike most of the wives of the khalifs, was as legendary a spender as her husband. She would serve guests with only gold and silver utensils encrusted with jewels. She is said to have spent $2,500,000 on a pilgrimage to Mecca. Zubaydah set the tone for Arab society. She was the first to ornament her shoes with precious stones. At the wedding of her granddaughter she gave the bridal couple a gold tray with a thousand pearls "of unique size." The groom's father gave important guests a special robe and a ball of musk, in which was a slip of paper naming an estate, a slave, a team of horses, or some other unusual gift. Lesser guests were presented with gold or silver coins or eggs of amber. And so it went, for dancing girls, singers, concubines, even slaves. Harun's concubines were said to have numbered in the thousands, many sent him by victorious generals. European boys, mainly Greek or Armenian, perfumed and adorned, were also favored. The money and the wealth rolled in from the inexhaustible provinces and dependencies, for it was a time of relative peace, and wealth begat wealth.

The rich lived hardly less well, and even middle-class life was more than adequate: The equivalent of $100,000 a year was considered a fair income. Houses were cooled by ice brought down from the Persian mountains. Tableware was of silver. Despite the Qur'anic prohibitions, alcohol was drunk publicly, and to excess. Harun's son al-Amin had three barges for excursions on the rivers, one in the shape of a lion, another a dolphin, and the third an eagle, each costing some $300,000.

Persian clothes, fine and costly, replaced the rough robes of the desert. The provinces and the outlands from Damascus to the Afghan mountains were looted for valuables—brocades from Fars, taffeta from Iran, damask from Damascus, pewter, glass (a Syrian specialty), stained glass, gold and silver, pearls, rubies, and lapis lazuli from beyond the Oxus, turquoise, antimony, marble, sulphur, and for commercial uses, paper, pitch, tar, and mercury. Some items in Iraq's ordinary daily use such as glass and paper were discovered later by the Crusaders and taken home as curiosities. Trade extended everywhere—to Europe, to Russia (Arab coins have been found in archaeological digs in Finland and Russia), to India, to ports on the Mediterranean—and included silks, perfumes, porcelain, dyes, spices, ivory, and slaves. Agriculture flourished. The Tigris and Euphrates delta was drained, new canals were dug, and crops of barley, wheat, rice, and dates were bountiful.

With literacy common and not the privilege of a few, social

standards were high. There were 27,000 public baths. Medicine and pharmacy was a Baghdad specialty. There were eight hundred doctors, licensed to weed out the quacks. Foreign medical works from the East were translated into Arabic, and Arabic medicine had such a sound standing that Western medicine was based on it for centuries, either on Arabic versions of Greek knowledge, or on the Arabs' own discoveries.

When Harun al-Rashid died in 809, his son Muhammad al-Amin ordered an inventory of the khalif's belongings. The secretaries and storekeepers spent four months inspecting and counting the treasures. To show the kind of things a khalif might possess, and to give an idea of his wealth, here is the inventory.

    4,000 embroidered robes
    4,000 silk cloaks lined with sable, mink, and other furs
  10,000 shifts and shirts
  10,000 caftans
    2,000 underdrawers of various kinds
    4,000 turbans
    1,000 hoods
    1,000 capes of various types
    5,000 kerchiefs
     500 pieces of velvet
 100,000 mithqals [a mithqal equaled about 4.25 grams] of musk
 100,000 mithqals of ambergris
    1,000 baskets of Indian aloes
    1,000 precious china vessels
           many kinds of perfumes
           gems valued by the jewelers at four million dinars
           [a dinar was worth about ten dollars]
 500,000 dinars

  1,000 jeweled rings
  1,000 Armenian carpets
  4,000 curtains
  5,000 cushions
  5,000 pillows
  1,500 silk carpets
    100 silk rugs
  1,000 silk cushions and pillows
    300 Maysani carpets
  1,000 Darabjirdi carpets
  1,000 cushions with silk brocade
  1,000 inscribed silk cushions
  1,000 silk curtains
    300 silk brocade curtains
    500 Tabari carpets
  1,000 Tabari cushions
  1,000 pillows (mirfada type)
  1,000 pillows (mikhadda type)
  1,000 ewers
    300 stoves
  1,000 candlesticks
  2,000 brass objects of various kinds
  1,000 belts
 10,000 decorated swords
 50,000 swords for the guards and the pages
150,000 lances
100,000 bows
  1,000 special suits of armor
 50,000 common suits of armor
 10,000 helmets
 20,000 breastplates
150,000 shields
  4,000 special saddles
 30,000 common saddles
  4,000 pairs of half-boots, most lined with sable, mink, and

other kinds of fur, with a knife and a kerchief in
each half-boot
4,000 pairs of socks
4,000 small tents with their appurtenances
  150 marquees

It was a productive land, except for the unrelenting desert,
and it could draw upon the entire kingdom—and Byzantium
and India as well—for its supplies. Wheat from Egypt, millet
from Arabia, rice from the Jordan Valley, sheep and goats
from the steppes and from Palestine, fish from the Red Sea and
the Gulf of Persia, raisins from Jerusalem, olives from Pal-
myra, apples from Syria, spices from the Far East, and at
home and in Persia the rose gardens for the petals which gave
a special flavor to Arab cooking. In the Arabian desert the
tribes had existed on mutton, barley, dates, and sheep's milk.
In Iraq they could draw upon the ancient traditions of Persian
cuisine for an exotic fare, and all but the poor ate well. There
were beans and lentils, chickpeas, olives, figs, dates, grapes,
quinces, walnuts, almonds, pomegranates, apricots, lemons and
limes, walnuts, pistachios, almonds, and jams of many fruits.
Much of what is today considered Middle Eastern cooking was
originally Persian, adapted by the Arabs and carried along by
the Turks (who added a few of their own recipes) in their
conquests of Cappadocia and Anatolia, Greece and the Balkans. An old document describes a meal—not a banquet—for
a Sassanian king as being made of "hot and cold meats," rice
jelly, stuffed vine leaves, chicken marinated in spices and
grilled on a spit, and meat fried in butter and covered with a
sauce. The king was also served a "Greek" pudding (but it
also sounds Indian) of rice, sugar, honey, and milk. Another
course was salted mutton with pomegranate juice, served with

eggs. Also there was young kid and beef cooked with spinach and vinegar.

The Arabs (they may have picked this up from the Persians, though it sounds like something from their desert days) liked the fat of a sheep's tail, a certain kind of sheep having such a heavy tail that a little wagon had to be placed under it to carry it. We hear of Baghdad dishes rich in mutton fat with meat, fruit, nuts, vegetables, and poached eggs, all in a single pot. One-pot cooking was common, and meat was a common ingredient; today a general overgrazing of the Arab lands from Morocco to the Iraqi delta, with the consequent shortage of sheep and goats, and widespread poverty mean vegetarian meals for the general populace.

A few years ago an English Arabist, Professor A. J. Arberry, discovered an old Iraqi cookbook by a man called al-Baghdadi, after his natal city. The author gives a simple dish, called Makhfiya.

> Cut red meat into thin strips about four fingers long. . . .
> Put it into the oil [he doesn't say how much], with a dirham
> [roughly ⅛ ounce] of salt and fine ground dry coriander,
> and fry lightly until brown. Then cover with water, adding
> green coriander leaves, cinnamon bark, a handful of chick-
> peas, and a handful of onion chopped fine. Boil, and remove
> the scum. Now mince [more] red meat fine and make into
> kebabs [meatballs] with seasonings. Take hard-boiled eggs,
> remove the whites, and place the yolks in the middle of the
> kebabs, and place in the pan. When nearly cooked, add fine-
> ground cumin, pepper, mastic [gum arabic], and ginger.
> Take [more] eggs and beat well; remove the strips of meat,
> dip them while still hot in the egg, and return them to the
> pot. Do this two or three times, until the slices have a coat-
> ing of egg, and finally return them to the pot. When the

 In the patriarchal society of the Middle East, the men often spend endless hours drinking tiny cups of sweet, thick coffee, while the women care for the children, work in the fields and go to the U.N. Relief Center (if they are poor) for rations.

liquid has evaporated, sprinkle a dirham of fine-ground cinnamon, spray with a little rose water, and leave to settle over the fire [it must be a low flame] for an hour.

Al-Baghdadi wrote that he "loved eating above all pleasures." He traveled all over the Arab world in his search for gastronomic happiness. He was enthralled by the dishes of the Egyptians. He remarked that most of their stews are not much different from those elsewhere but—

> Their sweet stews are of a singular kind, for they cook a chicken with all sorts of sweet substances. Here is how they prepare the food: they boil a fowl, then put it in a julep [a mixture of water with syrup or sugar], place under it crushed hazelnuts or pistachio nuts, poppy seeds or rose hips, and cook the whole until it thickens. Then they add spices and remove it from the fire.

Another cookbook, the *Kitab al Wusla il al Habib*, lists over five hundred recipes for chicken. There were numerous cookbooks, manuals of etiquette, and other works designed to raise the standards of people newly come from the provinces, or of people suddenly affluent. And the upper classes were constantly searching for new thrills, new experiences. Al-Baghdadi's book seems to have been one of the most popular, so I will give a few more of his recipes, which are still in use today in the Middle East and can be done fairly easily in a Western kitchen. He uses yogurt, or *laban* as the Arabs call it, which was often eaten with garlic or fruit or honey, or used as a marinade for beef, lamb, or chicken along with spices.

NA'NA MUKHALAL (a vinegar dressing)
Take fresh, large-leafed mint and strip the leaf from the stalk. Wash and dry in the shade, sprinkle with aromatic herbs. If desired add celery leaves and quarters of peeled

garlic. Put into a glass bottle and cover with good vinegar, colored with a little saffron. Let stand until the mint has absorbed the sourness of the vinegar so that the latter has lost its sharpness, then serve.

BAID MUTAJJAN

A specifically Middle Eastern recipe that al-Baghdadi offers is fried, hard-boiled eggs with spices, called *baid mutajjan*. (He uses many hard-boiled eggs in his cuisine.) The recipe is simple: The eggs are boiled, shelled and peeled, and fried whole in oil, then rolled in, or sprinkled with, a mixture of equal parts of ground coriander and cumin (a teaspoon of each would be sufficient) and a half-part of ground cinnamon, and salted to taste. Such spiced eggs are still sold by street vendors in some of the Arab countries.

Here is another egg recipe from al-Baghdadi.

BAID MASUS

Take fresh sesame oil, place in a saucepan and heat; add chopped celery. Add some fine, ground coriander, cumin, and cinnamon, plus some mastic [gum arabic]; put in vinegar as needed, and color with a little saffron. When [the mixture] is thoroughly boiling, bread eggs and drop in whole. When set, remove.

MASGOUF

The inland Arabs used much salt fish, though there was a popular freshwater variety, charboute, found in the Tigris and Euphrates, which was (and is) grilled and smoked over a charcoal fire to make a popular dish called *masgouf*. The fish was split open, cleaned and salted inside and out, and either left in the sun to dry or buried in the desert sand or the river mud flats. Salted it was called *fessih*. Here are some of al-Baghdadi's recipes for salt fish, though they work as well with fresh fish. Before the fish is used with the recipe, it has to be soaked at least twelve hours in several changes of cold water, then cooked briefly in fresh cold water and drained.

MALIH BI-LABAN

Take salted fish, wash, and clean. . . . Fry in sesame oil. Remove while hot and drop into milk [seasoned with] chopped garlic. Sprinkle with fine-ground cumin, coriander, and cinnamon. May be served either hot or cold.

MALIH BI KHALL WA-KHARDAL

Fry [the fish] in sesame oil. Remove from the frying pan and place in vinegar with fine-ground mustard and coriander. Color the vinegar with a little saffron.

The Persian influence shows in this recipe for lamb and apricots, mishmish.

MISHMISHIYA

Cut fat meat into small pieces, put into a saucepan with a little salt, and cover with water. Boil and remove the scum. Add chopped onions; add seasonings—coriander, cumin, mastic, cinnamon, pepper, and ginger, all ground well. Soak dried apricots in water, rinse, and boil lightly in a separate pan until soft. Drain and press through a sieve. Add the juice to the saucepan to form a broth. Take [blanched] sweet almonds, grind them fine, moisten with apricot juice and add to the saucepan. A pinch of saffron may be added for color. Spray the stew with a little rose water, wipe the sides of the pan with a clean towel [for a neat appearance], and leave to settle over a [low] fire, then remove.

The flat unleavened bread of the early agriculturists on the fringe highlands of Mesopotamia (see page 33) took on a new dimension with the regular use of yeast and became a staple all across the Middle East. Yeast made the bread (cooked in large, even huge, ovens usually operated on a communal basis by one of the village families) form a "pocket," which collapses when the loaf is removed from the oven heat. This bread is known by many names, among them *khubz*, *chammi* and *pita*. The standard recipe is virtually the same as that for the ancient stone-cooked breads, with the addition of yeast. In the past some dough was saved from each batch to mix with the next, and so on, but today it is easier to use commercial yeast.

KHUBZ, CHAMMI, or PITA
3½ to 4 cups of unbleached white flour
1⅓ cup of warm water
1 package of dried yeast
1 tablespoon of salt

In a large bowl dissolve the yeast in the warm water with about a cup of flour. Let it stand about five minutes. Add the salt, stir, and add the rest of the flour. Mix thoroughly, turn out on a floured board, and knead for five minutes, so that the dough takes on the traditional, spongy, coherent form. Divide into six equal balls; roll in flour lightly and let stand for half an hour covered with a light towel. Now roll each ball out flat into a round of about seven inches in diameter. Let the loaves stand covered for another half hour.

Turn your oven on to the highest possible heat. When it seems to have reached its hottest, place the loaves on ungreased, unfloured baking sheets (you will need two) and place on the *floor* of the oven. Bake about six minutes and check. The loaves should have puffed up. The bread will be ready when it is slightly tinged with brown. Do not overcook. Usually eight to ten minutes is sufficient. It may be wise to experiment with one loaf first. Cool before eating.

As we have seen with other peoples, other civilizations in the fabulous land of the two rivers, everything bears the seeds of

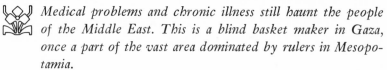 *Medical problems and chronic illness still haunt the people of the Middle East. This is a blind basket maker in Gaza, once a part of the vast area dominated by rulers in Mesopotamia.*

its own death. The khalifs of Islam became so enamored of their powers, of the richness and profligacy of their lives, that they ruled less and less, leaving that unpleasant task to their wazirs, most often Persians, but later Turks. The dizzying heights of Harun's century ended in a fall in the fortunes of the powerful and wide-flung khalifate. Harun's sons, al-Amin and al-Ma'mun, respectively the Honest and the Trusted One, the first the son of an Arab mother, the other the son of a Persian, entered into a futile fraternal struggle upon the death of their father in 809. Al-Amin, the most aggressive and for a while the most powerful, proclaimed himself khalif, even though the father had favored the half-Persian son. In the ensuing struggle it was the Arab side—for al-Amin was Arab through both parents—which won. Al-Ma'mun retired into the provinces to bide his time.

Then, in 812, after al-Amin had served but three years as khalif, he faced a major attack by his half-brother. Al-Ma'mun's armies besieged Baghdad. The khalif, a frivolous, wine-loving womanizer, had lost most of his popularity, and many of his troops had deserted. Al-Ma'mun proclaimed himself the true khalif, to the cheers of the common people. The siege of Baghdad must have been frightening. Al-Amin's men and officers were starving and half-naked, without proper armor; most of their weapons were gone and they were reduced to using shields of woven palm leaves and wood-tipped lances. Yet they held out for fourteen months while al-Ma'mun's general battered away at the ninety-foot-high walls of the City of Peace. When the attackers finally broke through, they found Baghdad in ruins, its streets jammed with bodies. The mosques were closed, and not only the remnants of the army but the survivors of the civilian population were near death from starvation and exhaustion. Al-Amin held out for another three days in the citadel before surrendering, being promised safe conduct by one of the enemy generals. But as he was being taken across the Tigris some of the victorious troops from another—rival—general's command cut off his head and sent it to al-Ma'mun. Another version of his death, more in keeping with his character, but probably not to be trusted, says that his enemies found him in the midst of a party on one of his barges and murdered him.

Baghdad, once the pride of the Arab world and the literal center of civilization, lay in ruins. The victorious new khalif, al-Ma'mun, moved to Persia while the capital was being rebuilt. Since his mother and wife were Persians, his bias was Persian. His subjects, or at least the Arabs, now feared that he was becoming not only Iranized but heretical, for Al-Ma'mun had moved from being an orthodox Sunni to the more mystical and esoteric Shi'ism.

As an example of what the change to Shi'ism meant, al-Ma'mun ordered that the official robes throughout the empire be changed from black, the Abbasid color, to green, the Shi'a color. In Baghdad, the people proclaimed a new khalif, an Arab uncle of al-Ma'mun's, a doddering, inefficient old man who lost the support of the people after two years.

The Persianizing of the khalifate brought the empire close to civil war. Now al-Ma'mun saw his chance. Thoroughly Arabized again, at least in public, he returned to Baghdad. He put down incipient uprisings, pardoned rebels in a grand gesture—changed the colors back to black—and to enforce Sunni orthodoxy created an inquisition to stamp out heresy. The better side of his character resulted in the establishing of a period of high learning; he founded schools and universities, inviting scholars, no matter what their race or religion—Greeks, Christians, Jews, Zoroastrians, Egyptians, Phoenicians—to his court for one of the most creative periods in the history of the khalifate.

We need not examine every khalif: We are interested in the sweep of history, and some exemplars here and there. The khalifate, once proud of its strict adherence to the firm doctrines, almost puritanical in execution, of the Prophet, quickly degenerated into weakness and licentiousness. By the end of the century the khalifs barely ruled outside the environs of Baghdad. In 902 the Khalif Muqtadir—he was the eleventh since al-Ma'mun, who had died in 833—who had ruled twenty-four years in drunkenness, was twice deposed by Turkish mercenaries, who finally cut off his head and placed it on a spear outside the palace. At one point there were three Abbasid khalifs still living but deposed by their wazirs, each of the three having been blinded by a successor, who deprived him of wealth and crown alike.

10

DIGGING UP
THE PAST

ABOUT THE MIDDLE OF THE SEVENTH CENTURY B.C. ASHURBANI-
pal, king of Nineveh, general, looter of other people's empires
(Egypt, Susa), and scholar, ordered his savants to scour the
world as he knew it—or controlled it—in search of ancient
documents to add to his already impressive collection of historical records and older works, hymns, poems, and scientific
and religious texts. Among the ancient seats of learning to be
plundered of their libraries and other documents (mostly on
clay) were Babylon, Nippur, and Uruk. Shamash-shum-ukin,
Ashurbanipal's brother (perhaps even his twin), was king of
Babylon; a shrewd plotter, Ashurbanipal turned on his brother
and drove him to suicide. Uruk, of course, as we have seen,
was the home of the warrior-god-king Gilgamesh, whose exploits were celebrated two thousand years later from Mesopotamia to the shores of the Mediterranean. Vast quantities of

the old texts, written in various languages, were found and brought to the royal palace at Nineveh to be cataloged, and if necessary translated. To many was added the legend, "Written down according to the original and collated in the palace of Ashurbanipal, King of the World, King of Assyria." Despite his rather commonplace bloodthirsty nature, he must have been a remarkable man.

An unusual feature of Ashurbanipal's time was an interest in history and literature of the past. The king could boast that he had brought back to Uruk a statue of the goddess Ishtar (under her form of Nanaya) that the Elamites had carried off 1,635 years before. There was a special interest in Sargon of Akkad, who had lived in the twenty-fourth century B.C., and who had united Sumer in the south with the north, the first time that so much of Mesopotamia had been brought together. Texts concerning Sargon were collected and put into libraries. At Ur, one of the great Sumerian cities, the Assyrian governor in his restoration of the town came across various early Sumerian texts and had them translated and exhibited in the temple.

Not long afterward Ashurbanipal's empire fell apart. Revolts by Egyptians, a general decay of administrative forces, the shutting off by barbarians of the supply of horses upon which the Assyrian army relied, necessitating an expedition to put down the nomads, and other setbacks are some of the causes. Ashurbanipal died about 626 B.C. One of his successors, Sin-shar-ishkin, is the king who is credited with having lost control of what was left of Assyria. A traitorous ally of the king betrayed him by going over to a new and previously unknown enemy, the Medes, an Iranian tribe, who stormed Nineveh. As the city went up in flames, Sin-shar-ishkin, together with his wives, committed suicide, amid a notable lack of mourning. The Hebrew Prophet Nahum chanted: "Nineveh is laid waste; who will bemoan her?" It was a rich city, or at least the kings were rich. Greek historians, who were not always reliable but enjoyed a reputation for being gullible, stated that the treasure of Sin-shar-ishkin consisted of one hundred and fifty golden couches, each with a matching golden table, and ten million talents of gold, one hundred million talents of silver, and a great amount of expensive clothing, including robes of purple, the most costly color. It is difficult to give ancient currencies in contemporary terms, but about the time of the Greek historians the talent was worth roughly $1,250, if not double that.

But Nineveh was gone. The ruins of the great city and its vast libraries, with their clay tablets stored in jars marked by palm-leaf inscriptions, disappeared under the dust and the silt of time, and the ruins stood forlorn and unlamented.

The loss of an ancient city was commonplace. I must mention the loss of another, Persepolis, for both it and Nineveh have a special role to play in this chapter. In the fourth century B.C. the world-conquerer Alexander the Great, whose empire at its greatest extent ran from Macedonia across Turkey and Mesopotamia and into western India, captured the great Persian city of Persepolis. (The name means "Persian City" in Greek.) In Persepolis, which is now in ruins, is a great building which had been the residence of two of the most famous Persian rulers, Darius and Xerxes, best known for their ill-fated attempts at invading Greece (in 490 and 480 B.C., respectively). The Greeks destroyed the palace of the emperors under Alexander's orders, given, according to a Greek historian, "during a drinking bout when he was no longer in control of his wits." Another Greek gives a more interesting, but possibly less reliable, version of the story. The Greek courtesan Thais, in the frenzy of her dance before Alexander and his generals, hurled a flaming torch at the wooden columns of the palace (many were of stone, however), which caught on fire. The Greeks, all drunk, joined in the fun and the palace was partially destroyed. However, enough of the building remained standing over the centuries for the Arabs to use it. Eventually weather and age brought its final collapse, and only nomadic sheepherders and their flocks could be found in the ruins.

Travelers through Persia picked up many fragments of statuary and other art, some of which were sent back to Europe. In the years between 1760 and 1767 a German scholar, Karsten Niebuhr, visited Persepolis and, fascinated by the ruins and the monumental sculpture, painstakingly copied down some of the inscriptions. However no one was able to decipher them at the time.

Old Persian texts had been reaching Europe during this period, and Western scholars had begun to study the language in various forms—modern, classical, and medieval. One of the most important aids to a breakthrough in deciphering the mystery of the Persepolis inscriptions resulted from someone seeing old manuscript pages belonging to a small religious community, the Parsis, a group of Persian exiles who had been living in India for over a thousand years. In 1754 a twenty-year-old Frenchman, Anquetil-Duperron, saw a few of the pages and decided he would like to visit the Parsis and study their scriptures. In the eighteenth century travel halfway around the world was not easily accomplished alone. In order to get safely to India Anquetil-Duperron had to join the French East India Company as a common soldier. After his four-year enlistment period was completed, he was free to devote his time to the Parsis, though his work was slowed by illness and the initial distrust of the community elders. But eventually he was able to bring home the complete text of the Avesta, the Parsi equivalent of the Bible and the Qur'an. The Avesta, however, was not written in Old Persian but in various forms of another archaic language called Zend, which resembled Persian. At first Anquetil-Duperron's Avesta was called a fake, for no European scholar had heard either of the Avesta or Zend, but its value was soon realized and the work was added to the increasing store of Middle Eastern knowledge.

At the time that Anquetil-Duperron was persuading the Parsis to let him copy down their most sacred and secret scriptures, and Niebuhr was tracing the inscriptions at Persepolis—the period shortly before the French and American Revolutions—virtually all that was known of the Middle East, of Mesopotamia, came either from the Bible, which presented the Hebrew version of events, or from the writings of Greek and Roman classical authors, who most often had to rely upon secondary and tertiary and often inaccurate and exaggerated versions obtained from travelers. But shortly the entire world of Middle Eastern history was to be opened up to mankind, to be followed by a century and a half of archaeological explorations unique in their findings.

The inscriptions at Persepolis had been carved in cuneiform, a type of writing made by pressing a wedge into wet clay (cuneus means "wedge" in Latin) or by chiseling similar marks into hard stone. Soon even this impenetrable mystery was solved. In 1802 G. F. Grotefend, a twenty-seven-year-old German schoolteacher who had made a bet with friends he could decipher cuneiform, had made a first, tentative translation of a copy of part of the Persepolis inscriptions.

Grotefend's approach to cuneiform was highly original and imaginative, for the texts, which everyone seemed to agree resembled a collection of bird tracks, had to be considered from many aspects. Grotefend's first report required pages of com-

The Sumerians developed the cuneiform system of alphabetizing sounds about five thousand years ago, and soon turned simple diagrams into a highly complex and accurate means of writing. Originally the symbols were quite pictorial—the sun, a human face, a fish, etc.—but they quickly became abstract.

plicated explanation, and I can give only a few of the basic
problems. First of all, did the columns, which were terribly
crowded with the symbols, read up and down, or across, and
in which direction? For it was known that many alphabets did
not follow the left to right pattern of the West. Grotefend
decided that the texts ran just as they did in European works.
Also, after working on the problem, he realized that not one
but three languages were involved. The highly educated
Grotefend knew much history, especially what had been
gleaned from the Bible and the classical writers. He knew that
the Persian King Cyrus had attacked and conquered the Babylonians about 540 B.C. and that from then on it was Persia, not
Babylon, that dominated the Middle East and challenged the
Egyptians. It was consequently a sensible deduction that part
of the inscription was in the language of the conquerors—
Persian—and that it was most likely the central column, with
the other languages (which turned out to be Elamite, an Iranian tongue akin to Persian, and the Semitic tongue used by
the Assyrians and Babylonians) on the flanks. Proceeding by
logical steps he then deduced that certain phrases must apply
to the rulers, and they would be repeated with but minor
changes.

> X, GREAT KING OF KINGS, KING OF A AND B,
> SON OF Y, GREAT KING OF KINGS . . .

and so on. He was not at all surprised to find similar clumps
of cuneiform inscriptions. The first word would probably be
the ruler's name, and one of the others the word "king." He
now began to work on the most common of the clumps, drawing upon his knowledge of the Persian dynasties.

> I began to check through the royal successions to find out
> which names most nearly fitted the inscriptional characters.

They could not be Cyrus and Cambyses, because the two names in the inscriptions did not have the same initial letter, nor could they be Cyrus and Artaxerxes, because the first of these names, relative to the characters, was too short, the second too long. There were no names to choose from but Darius and Xerxes, and they fitted so easily that I had no doubt about making the right choice. This correspondence was clinched by the fact that in the son's inscription the father's name had the sign of royalty beside it, whereas this character was lacking in the father's inscription. This observation was confirmed by all the Persepolitan inscriptions.

Grotefend had been working with the Greek versions of the royal names, which are slightly different from the Persian. He now turned to the Avesta, where he found true Persian forms of the names, and was thus able to correct his translations. The Greek "Darius," as both the Avesta revealed and Grotefend found from the inscriptions, was spelled *Darayawaush*. The Greek "Xerxes" was, in old Persian, *Khshayarsha*. Grotefend now had identified over a dozen cuneiform symbols, and with these he could figure out some other words; however, he was unable to translate the text in its entirety. But a beginning had been made. Other scholars, among them the Frenchman Émile Burnouf and the German Christian Lassen, proceeded from Grotefend's initial work and were able to revise and improve upon it, their research being published in 1836.

The next year a new beginning was made by an Englishman, one Major Henry Creswicke Rawlinson, who was totally ignorant of the work done by Grotefend, Burnouf, and Lassen. Rawlinson was an unusual person, a true character, a typical nineteenth-century adventurer-scholar-diplomat, highly intelligent, formidably educated, imaginative and fearless in the field, and willing to go where no other European had ever gone, where even the natives dared not go, taking incredible risks to gain information about and insights into other cultures, whether present or past.

Rawlinson was born in 1810, and like many young men of that period, in England and on the continent, he saw his future in Asia. At the age of seventeen he joined the British East India Company, the commercial organization which had won the privilege from the British Crown of exploiting all the Indies and Asia it could control, vying not only with upstart native princes who resented foreign intervention in their affairs, but with the French, Dutch, and Portuguese, who had similar companies and similar aims. Rawlinson arrived in India as an officer cadet, but ambition, coupled with the high mortality rate of fellow officers, quickly made him a major, and at the age of twenty-three, along with other members of the company, he was transferred to Persia to help organize the Persian army along modern lines.

But there were other things to occupy his time and energies besides the shah's military machine. Rawlinson became interested in cuneiform inscriptions, and by chance came across copies of some clay tablets that Burnouf had worked from. But Rawlinson was ignorant of the efforts of others in the field. Nevertheless, starting afresh he went much further in his deciphering, and by a process similar to that worked out by Grotefend, translated the names of three Persian kings and four other names, plus several ordinary words. It was not until the results of this brief excursion into the past had been published that Rawlinson learned of Grotefend's work a generation previous. Now he sought out cuneiform on a grand scale. He had heard of a curious place known as Bagistana (or Behustan), "the landscape of the gods," where a road ran through a rocky valley, on the sides of which were both strange carvings and strange inscriptions. So to Bagistana he went. Just as the reports had said, Rawlinson found that on the walls of the surrounding cliffs, 160 feet above the roadway, were the carvings and the inscriptions, huge figures of kings and their armies cut into the stone and cuneiform by the yard. One of the kings, he soon learned, was none other than Darius, leaning on his bow, with one foot on a prostrate figure, the Magus Gaumata, who had posed as the brother of the emperor Cambyses, now dead, and had raised a revolt against the royal house. Accompanying the king were two of his nobles, in armor and war gear, and before him were the nine "Kings of Lies" he had vanquished, now shown with their hands bound and their necks tied with rope. Darius had put the usurper Gaumata to death and reestablished the family dynasty. Fourteen columns of inscriptions ran along the sides and bottom of the great monument in some unknown language. But what one was it? And how was Rawlinson to copy it down—for he realized that trying to record such a strange conglomeration of carved characters from such a distance could only result in numerous errors.

With little thought for the many dangers involved he scaled the cliff from the back and let himself down precariously by rope to make notes of the central text—which he decided was Old Persian, the language he had been working in. It was a most dangerous undertaking. He was able to make a fair copy and a translation, which went like this:

KING DARAYAWAUSH GIVES NOTICE THUS:

YOU WHO IN FUTURE DAYS

WILL SEE THIS INSCRIPTION BY ORDER

WRIT WITH HAMMER UPON THE CLIFF,

WHO WILL SEE THESE HUMAN FIGURES HERE—

EFFACE, DESTROY NOTHING.
TAKE CARE, SO LONG AS YOU HAVE SEED,
TO LEAVE THEM UNDISTURBED.

It was a major success, getting this scrap of Old Persian cuneiform. Official duties interfered with further detailed investigation of Bagistana, for Rawlinson was sent to Afghanistan in 1839. During the British occupation of Afghanistan, which meant tiring and unceasing war with the Afghanis, Rawlinson, as he complained, "had no alternative but the abandonment of antiquarian research." But four years later he was transferred to Baghdad as the British consul, and he was able to visit Bagistana again the following year. Meanwhile he was trying to catch up with the flood of new copies of cuneiform texts and their translations that had appeared. In Baghdad he dove into his studies with energy, analyzing with the help of Sanskrit and Zend, two languages he had added to his storehouse, "nearly every word of the Cuneiform inscriptions hitherto in Persian." Though he was polite to the work of his predecessors and contemporaries, he still did not think much of it.

> The translations of Professor Grotefend and of Saint-Martin [a minor Orientalist] are altogether erroneous and merit no attention whatever. The memoir of M. Burnouf on the inscriptions of Hamadan is confined to the illustration of twenty short lines of writing . . . the nature of the inscriptions has necessarily rendered the labours of the Paris secretary, ample and erudite as they are, deficient in historical interest; and the faulty condition of his alphabet has, moreover, led him into several important errors of translation. . . . In a list which exhibits the titles of twenty-four of the most celebrated nations of ancient Asia, he has correctly deciphered ten only of the names.

> Of Professor Lassen's translations . . . he is not, I think, without error in his reading and appropriation of these names. . . . he has also in many cases misunderstood both the etymology of the words and the grammatical structure of the language. . . .

Having disposed of his rivals—Rawlinson seems to act as if he were in his own war with upstart natives in dealing with other scholars—he proceeds to state, without a pretense of modesty:

> In the present case, then, I do put forth a claim to originality, as having been the first to present to the world a literal, and, as I believe, a correct grammatical translation of nearly two hundred lines of Cuneiform writing, a memorial of the time of Darius Hystaspes, the greater part of which is in so perfect a state as to afford simple and certain grounds for a minute orthographical and etymological analysis. . . .

Rawlinson, of course, as everyone knew, had obtained his material by dangling like some puppet from ropes precariously guided by his assistant atop the Bagastana cliff, while he carefully traced each scratch of cuneiform. Everyone else had stayed on the ground, or had worked in the seclusion of the library from copies of tablets sent home from the field.

Rawlinson obtained some new, more accurate material from a Dane and a Russian who had been to Persepolis, but there was no further work to be accomplished except by returning to the cliffs of Bagastana and tackling more of the inscriptions.

> I succeeded in copying the whole of the Persian writing at that place [Bagastana], and a very considerable portion also of the Median and Babylonian transcripts. I will not speak of the difficulties or dangers of the enterprise.

He then adds modestly, "They are such as any person with

ordinary nerves may successfully encounter," only to qualify
this immediately.

> But they are such, at the same time, as have alone prevented
> the inscriptions from being long ago presented to the public
> by some of the numerous travelers who have wistfully con-
> templated them from a distance.

But Rawlinson's work did not go unchallenged. It was an
age when oriental studies attracted the best scholars in Europe,
and the literature of all of Asia, from Arabia and Mesopotamia
to India, China, and Japan, was flooding the university jour-
nals and presses. Many previously unknown languages and cultures, literatures, and subjects had been taken up. Perhaps it was
Rawlinson's brashness that turned the scholars against him. But
he had rescued not only the Old Persian, but the texts of the
two other languages, which he called Class II and Class III. A
Dane, Niels Westergaard, who had visited many of the sites
and had discussed the inscriptions with Rawlinson, solved
Class II inscriptions with only moderate difficulty, for this language, Elamite, was related to Old Persian. Class III presented
a far more formidable problem, for each sign, as the scholars
soon realized, had multiple meanings, standing, perhaps, for a
letter (as with the Western alphabet) or for a word or group
of words, that is, as an ideogram (as in Chinese). There was no
clear-cut guide. Then a Frenchman, Paul Émile Botta, working
at a site in northern Mesopotamia called Kuyunjik (it turned
out to be the notorious Nineveh), made a fortuitous discovery: nearly a hundred clay tablets of word lists in two languages, Sumerian and Assyrian. Though both languages were
unknown, the fact that the cuneiform of the Old Persian was
fairly much the same as that of the Sumerian soon led
to the deciphering of the Assyrian, and then to the trans-

lating of the Class III texts of the rocky walls of Bagastana. Rawlinson was sent home on leave for two years. He presented his collection of cuneiform tablets and other rare antiquities to the British Museum, which in turn gave him a grant to continue excavations begun under British auspices in northern Mesopotamia. He retired from field work at the age of forty-five, but lived to the fine old age of eighty-five, active in both oriental studies and diplomatic affairs.

In 1826 Paul Émile Botta, a twenty-one-year-old Frenchman (he was the son of an Italian politician and academic) set off on a three-year voyage around the world. Botta immediately became interested in foreign lands, and instead of returning home after his three years abroad (he never made a full circle of the globe), he began to explore the eastern Mediterranean. On one occasion, in order to stay in the Middle East, he served as a doctor for an Arab sheik. Finally he entered the French diplomatic service. In 1836 Botta was appointed to serve in the consulate at Tripoli, a large town in Lebanon, which was then part of the Ottoman Turkish empire. Here he began to make trips across the Lebanese mountains and into the Tigris and Euphrates plain. In 1840 he was transferred to Mosul as the French consul. Mosul was a decrepit city on the middle Tigris with a bad reputation, due in part to its corrupt administration by the Ottoman Turks, whose governors were notorious for exploiting the Arabs. Claudius James Rich, an Englishman who had explored some ruins near Mosul, had written in his journal:

Mosul town is an evil city. By night robbers stalk untouched from house to house, and the time of rest and darkness is made fearful by the cracking of pistols and confused cries

of strife. By day, drunkenness and debauchery are openly
indulged in. The population is rotted by the foul distemper,
corrupted and rendered impotent by drink, stupefied and
besotted by vice.

By now Botta was skilled in dealing with Arabs and other
Middle Eastern peoples. He had learned Arabic and other
tongues, got along easily with Muslims, and had an insatiable
curiosity about the lands in which he was posted. He scoured
the bazaars for antiquities, and after them, the outlying villages
and towns, amassing a valuable collection of statuettes, vases,
pots, inscribed clay fragments, and other works. All the markets seemed to have such material, all obviously old, if not
ancient, much of kinds which he had not known of previously.
Where did such antiquities come from? But his question went
unanswered. No one among the local people would tell him
of the source of the finds, except that they lay "everywhere."
In 1808 Claudius James Rich had dug in a mound near Mosul
and had written out a manuscript of his work describing the
kind of things that Botta was being sold by the local Arabs.
But before Rich's efforts could be published he died of cholera,
at age thirty-three. Botta, who was impressed by Rich's work,
decided to dig in some of the same places, and so he turned to
a great mound lying across the river from Mosul. The place
was called Kuyunjik, after the small village that lay at its foot.

Working alone, with a small group of village laborers who
did the heavy digging, Botta probed for a year, here and there.
It was work that could drive a man mad, amid summer heat,
winter cold, strange winds, and spring floods. For this endless
digging, pits here, trenches there, revealed not one sign of a
major structure, no palace or temple, not even the ruins of a
house. All Botta found were some clay fragments and frac-
tured sculpture of unidentifiable origin.

An Arab had been watching him. (Botta seems to have been
a local joke, a Frank—as the Arabs called all foreigners—craz-
ily digging away, following up false leads, digging *anywhere*
anyone might suggest, seriously or in fun.) An Arab had been
watching. . . .

Dig here, dig there, Botta instructed his Arab workmen.
They would dig anywhere, for they were getting paid, and
they had no real idea of what the foreigner was looking for.

Squatting on his haunches, his hands stretched out across his
knees, the watching Arab suggested, told, persuaded the reluctant Botta, now exhausted after a year of fruitless digging,
that there was a better place, full of bricks, bricks with marks
on them, bricks by the thousands, bricks so many that only
Allah Himself knows their number. There were so many of
these fine bricks that the Arab had built his cooking oven out
of them, as had everyone in the village. Botta sent a couple of
his diggers over to the other village, about ten miles away. A
week passed. Botta had gotten rid of the pesty Arab, but his
workers had not returned. At last one of his men appeared.
He had a message. They had been digging where the Arab
said, and the first shovelsful of dirt showed part of a wall, so
they dug further, and they found more walls, the walls being
extraordinarily carved with the figures of kings and their armies, stone animals, inscriptions, many things being in bright
colors.

Botta immediately got on his horse and rode over to the
other town.

The discoveries were amazing. He found, for example, "a
symbolical half-length statue, representing the fore part of a
bull, human headed, projecting from the wall." The statue
was about sixteen-feet tall and carved out of a single block of
stone. A related statue showed "a winged personage with the

head of a bird." The walls between the statues were heavily ornamented. Botta had found a major treasure, the ancient site of Dur-sharrukin, a city planned and founded as his new capital by the Assyrian ruler Sargon II, who ruled from 721 to 705 B.C. But the Assyrians could not hold Dur-sharrukin, and it was abandoned to nomadic tribes who were hounding the Assyrians. The city was later captured by the Persians and renamed Khorsabad, after the Persian king.

In the field, Botta was running into many problems. He had talked the village chief, whose house stood in the way of the excavations, into moving out onto the plain, followed by the rest of the people. "The entire mound will thus be left at my disposal, and nothing shall escape my scrutiny," he wrote to a friend. But conditions overcame him, hardworking as he was. "The air of Khorsabad is particularly unhealthy," he continued in his letter, and he was obliged to stop work for some time. There had been a high turnover of his work gang and the foreman was dangerously ill. The summer heat was increasing. A worse problem had presented itself—once the bricks and the sculpture were exposed to the air, they began to disintegrate. Botta covered up what he could of the excavations.

> As for the others, I regret to say they will soon fall to atoms. Being no longer supported, the walls yield to the swelling [of the ground capillary movement of waters in the earth], the action of the sun reduces the surface to powder, and even now a considerable portion has disappeared.

Botta's letters to Paris brought the support of the government, the people, and the French press. He was sent assistants, including an artist to draw whatever might perish in the open. For three years Botta worked on the great city that lay at his feet as no city had ever lain at the feet of a conqueror. Despite heat and winter winds, the rains, the sickness of the work crews, desertions, and threats from the local Turkish governors, who could conceive only that Botta was looking for gold, the digging continued—the first major excavation of an ancient city.

The great palace lay bare: walls, streets, courtyards, magnificent sculptures, rich ornaments, massive portals, royal harems, and apartments. It was ancient royalty at its most magnificent again. But walls crumbled as they were exposed; great statues, carved in gypsum or alabaster, fragile materials, began to disintegrate.

Botta wanted to send some of the best pieces of sculpture to Paris. Rafts were loaded with magnificent specimens—the stone deities, winged figures, men-lions, victorious kings. Pushed out onto the Tigris, into water swifter than the boatmen could handle, the rafts spun around and tumbled their topheavy cargo into the river. A second set of sculptures was more cautiously loaded by the tireless Botta and survived the long trip down to Basra, where the pieces were put aboard an oceangoing vessel to be taken to the Louvre.

The work was too much for one man alone, and Botta was eventually joined by a committee of nine archaeologists who were to continue the excavations. Among them was a young Englishman, Austen Henry Layard, who was to find what Botta missed at Kuyunjik.

Layard was English, though born (in 1817) of French parents in Paris, but was educated in Italy, France, and Switzerland, and finally England. After a few years working in a solicitor's office in London, he took off for Ceylon with the intention of joining the civil service, the country then being a British col-

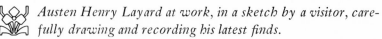 *Austen Henry Layard at work, in a sketch by a visitor, carefully drawing and recording his latest finds.*

ony. Though he had no money, Layard did not make the journey unprepared. He took up practical pursuits, like the use of
the compass and the sextant for "navigating" on the open deserts he expected to cross, the making of geological surveys,
first aid, the curing of tropical diseases, and learning new languages—Arabic and Persian primarily. He traveled overland
and went through tribal country, experiencing numerous adventures. He reached Mesopotamia in 1839, rather ragged and
showing signs of privation and exhaustion. At Mosul he abandoned the idea of searching for a post in Ceylon and decided
to stay in the Middle East. Mesopotamia was particularly attractive to him, for he had read the Arabian Nights stories and
was enchanted by the descriptions of life in the great medieval
courts of Baghdad and Persia.

> During the autumn of 1839 and winter of 1840, I had been
> wandering through Asia Minor, scarcely leaving untrod
> one spot hallowed by tradition, or unvisited one ruin con-
> secrated by history. I was accompanied by one no less curi-
> ous and enthusiastic than myself. We were both equally
> careless of comfort and unmindful of danger. We rode
> alone; our arms were our only protection; a valise behind
> our saddles was our wardrobe, and we tended our own
> horses, except when relieved from the duty by the hospit-
> able inhabitants of a Turcoman village or an Arab tent. Thus
> unembarrassed by needless luxuries, and uninfluenced by the
> opinions and prejudices of others, we mixed among the
> people. . . .

In March, 1840, Layard and his companian entered Mosul,
and then began to explore the surrounding desert, finding
mounds here and there which Layard knew were the burial
places of old cities. One huge pyramid particularly attracted
him. It was a site referred to by the Greek general Xenophon,

as he led his famous Ten Thousand across Mesopotamia to Turkey and then home. Layard remarked that "the ruins around it were those which the Greek general saw twenty-two centuries before, and which were even then the remains of an *ancient* city. . . . Tradition still points to the origin of the city, and by attributing its foundations to Nimrod, whose name the ruins now bear, connects it with one of the first settlements of the human race."

He was determined to investigate the ruins, but his pitiably small funds were almost gone, and he returned to Constantinople, where he found a temporary home at the British embassy. Layard immediately tried to interest the ambassador, Sir Stratford Canning Day, in the ruins near Mosul, but with no success. For five years Layard, hanging on at the embassy without a formal post but doing unofficial missions for the ambassador, talked and talked about the mysterious mounds. Finally Sir Stratford gave him the grand sum of sixty British pounds, a pitifully small sum even then. Yet Layard took off at once. He journeyed due east, crossing the Euphrates and reaching the Tigris in November, 1845. At the Tigris he found a small boat that would take him downstream to Mosul.

Arriving at last at the mound of Nimrod, he found the entire area in a state of rebellion against the local Turkish governor, an obsessed, evil, savage man, who had been looting the Arab populace through excessive taxation, executing people he disliked, or burning down their homes. Layard decided that secrecy was the best route. He announced that he was going boar hunting, bought himself a good rifle and a spear, hired a horse, and, alone, set off for the mound. By sheer good fortune he was accepted by a local sheik, who found him six men to dig for moderate wages.

Before the first morning's work had been finished, the diggers had excavated a long trench which led to some alabaster slabs, which turned out to be the interior walls of a palace. Soon the local pasha tried to intervene, having heard that Layard was searching for, and finding, gold statuettes of great value. Endless delays now took place, and the pasha tried to find out what treasures were being unearthed, and Layard attempted to continue without having the pasha stop him completely. At last the interference ended, for the pasha was arrested and imprisoned for his crimes against the people, and Layard was free to continue undisturbed.

Great discoveries were then made, the first being a huge creature, a winged lion of alabaster.

> It was in admirable preservation [wrote Layard]. The expression was calm, yet majestic, and the outline of the features showed a freedom and knowledge of art, scarcely to be looked for in the works of so remote a period.

More and more works were uncovered; thirteen pairs of winged bulls and lions; reliefs; rooms of palaces; walls; sculptured gigantic winged figures, some with the heads of eagles, others human; bas-reliefs; labyrinths of rooms; long lines of kings and their attendants carved on the walls; mystic trees; figures bearing tribute; enormous bulls. On and on the discoveries went. "We . . . are half inclined to believe that we have dreamed a dream, or have been listening to some tale of Eastern romance," Layard observed.

A few were packed up and shipped downstream by rafts turning and tottering in the river. But they escaped the sad fate of Botta's first load and arrived at Basra, where they were carefully loaded aboard ship to go to the British Museum, rival of the Louvre in the race to exploit the buried riches of the ancient world.

In 1849, Nimrod having been thoroughly looted of its massive treasures, Layard turned to the mound that had failed Botta for a year, the site at Kuyunjik. Layard was by now a professional, and understood the problems involved in digging. Instead of probing at chance here and there, he sank a deep shaft into the mound. At twenty feet he reached a layer of bricks, and was almost immediately rewarded with the discovery of a palace. He had found one of the greatest treasures of archaeology, the city of Nineveh, so thoroughly effaced by war and time that no clues had remained to its location.

However it was not Layard's luck to find the royal library that Ashurbanipal had so carefully assembled. That honor went to a Chaldean Christian, one Hormuzd Rassam, born in Mosul in 1826. He was one of Layard's assistants at the digs at Nimrod and Kuyunjik in 1849 and 1850, and when his superior went home to England, Rassam took over the excavations. He was well qualified for the task. When he was twenty-one he had been fortunate enough to be allowed to enter Oxford, a rare opportunity for someone who was not only not English but a native as well; in fact he was what the English so disparagingly called a "wog"—a "westernized oriental gentleman." After working at Kuyunjik, Rassam entered the service of the British diplomatic corps, being posted to Aden on the Arabian peninsula, at that point on the Red Sea where the peninsula virtually touches Africa. Two years later, in 1856, Rassam was made deputy resident, a unique honor for an Arab in His Majesty's service. Rassam ran into trouble in 1866 on a diplomatic mission to Abyssinia, where the tyrannical and brutal King Theodore had him arrested. Rassam spent two years in prison before General Napier, one of the wilder British

 Austen Henry Layard, atop the wall, directs the removal of a winged, semihuman beast from the Assyrian palace at Nineveh. Such figures were installed to protect the king from evil spirits. The sketch is by Layard himself; the statue was shipped to the British Museum in London.

commanders, was able to free him. Upon his release Rassam celebrated his escape by returning to his natal city, where he again entered into the excitement of digging in the surrounding ruins.

It was during the 1850s that Rassam discovered the library, with some twenty-to-thirty thousand clay cuneiform tablets. Rassam was in full charge—Layard had gone home in 1851— but Rassam had the misfortune of being a "native," so he did not receive the acclaim that the English and French diggers had. But he was as courageous as any of them, putting down workmen's rebellions (which were more than mere strikes), and as perceptive in his approach, and he made some of the most important finds of all. At the mound of Nimrod, which had already been well worked over, Rassam was still able to unearth a great temple 160 feet long by 96 feet wide. At the nearby mound of Balawat he found a temple built by Ashurbanipal, as well as part of a city. One of the prizes at Balawat was a gate almost twenty-two and a half feet high, with bronze plates running across double doors dating back to the time of the ninth-century King Shalmaneser, showing the Assyrians victorious in battle, with rows of prisoners tied together by the neck. Like the tablets, the bronzes were sent to the British Museum.

Though the tablets were among Rassam's earliest finds submitted to the Museum, they languished virtually ignored for almost a decade. Purely by chance a young Englishman named George Smith had been browsing through the thousands of tablets from Ashurbanipal's collection and had come across one particular group that was of special interest. On December 3, 1862, Smith appeared before the newly organized Society of Biblical Archaeology to read a paper that caused a sensation among both scientists and the general public. For Smith was proud to announce that he had discovered and deciphered tablets giving a version of a flood which showed a striking resemblance to the Great Deluge of the Bible. There were some lines missing—that was obvious—but there were enough in the account to bring sensational newspaper stories all over the world.

A London newspaper, the *Daily Telegraph*, offered to finance Smith on a field trip to Mesopotamia to see if he could find the missing lines. But more than a few lines dealing with the flood were lost. Even as he had been working on his translation of the cuneiform Smith realized that the flood portion was but part of a longer piece of work dealing with a warrior named Gilgamesh. In fact some of the other tablets in the Museum collection referred to "The Gilgamesh Cycle" much as contemporary poets might identify some more recent work. Researching further among the tablets Smith learned that the flood canto was but the eleventh of a total of twelve, each of about 300 lines.

Smith was very much unlike the other men who had explored and excavated Mesopotamia. He was singularly ill-equipped physically. He had little formal education and went to work as an engraver of banknotes. But the discoveries in the Middle East, so well reported in the press, intrigued him, and he spent much of his free time in the Assyrian department of the British Museum. He made the acquaintance of Rawlinson, who, impressed by the young man's intelligence and enthusiasm, introduced him to the directors. Smith began to publish brief articles dealing with antiquities, which gained him some notice among Assyriologists. Among the papers which attracted attention was the translation of an inscription about an eclipse of the sun in 763 B.C., and another about the Elamites' invasion of Babylon, at a date which Smith fixed at 2280 B.C.

With the fine sum of 1,000 guineas behind him, the money offered by the *Telegram*, Smith set off at the head of a small expedition to find the missing piece of the flood narrative. Now what is surprising is that Smith, either by luck, instinct, or a shrewd insight into the methods of archaeology, found the missing portion in a very short time, though, as he wrote, "the ground [was] so cut up by former excavations that it was difficult to secure good results without more extensive operations than my time or means would allow." He continued to excavate various areas, finding a number of tablets and other antiquities which the earlier diggers had missed. He telegraphed the results of his findings to the *Daily Telegraph*, with a translation of the missing lines, seventeen in all. But "from some error unknown to me, the telegram as published differs materially from the one I sent." Moreover his sponsors misunderstood another remark, that "the season [for excavations] is closing," and ordered him home, whereas he had wanted to stay to continue his work when conditions permitted. But he stayed anyway, now getting support from the British Museum, and he found unparalleled treasures before his funds dried up.

Smith was a marked departure from many of his predecessors, for they were too often enamored of the big find, the gigantic statue, the impressive wall frieze of king and nobles and the conquered, while Smith understood the value of such seemingly mundane items as the clay tablets, which revealed much more about the daily life of the ancient cities. On his last trip into the field, in 1876, Smith, never of a rugged enough constitution to withstand the heat and the rigors of work in the desert, contracted a fever and died at Aleppo, Syria, at age thirty-six. By the time of his death he had published twelve major books and numerous articles dealing with Mesopotamia and its ancient cities.

By the end of the century the world realized that the ancient Middle East meant far more than a few references in the Bible and the Greek classics: Its history was older, its cultures deeper and more complex, and, most interesting of all, hitherto unknown peoples, notably the Sumerians (but also the Hurrians, Hittites, Guti, Mitannians, and so on) had been discovered. Here on these mountain-rimmed, well-watered steppes and plains was truly the source of world civilization.

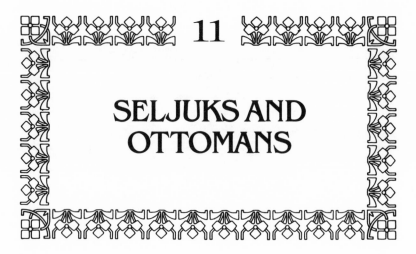

11

SELJUKS AND OTTOMANS

THE ARABS HAD DISINTEGRATED SO MUCH IN THE NINTH AND tenth centuries, losing their energies and abilities in their eloquent and lascivious pursuits of pleasure, that they could not resist a more powerful, barbaric, though less creative people—the Turks. For some two dozen centuries the Turks had been wandering about the steppes of Central Asia, from time to time bursting out of the oceanlike plains into China, India, Afghanistan, and Persia. They were commonly known as Turanians, after Turan, an area of Central Asia north of the Oxus River, where they seemed to be concentrated; the area is now called Turkestan. It was a "Turanian" soldier who killed the Iranian Prophet Zoroaster. The Turks were closely connected with the Scythians, the Huns, and the Mongols by blood, language, and custom. Attila the Hun and Genghis Khan (a Mongol) both spoke Turkish. As nomads, marauders, and traders the Turks had no written language and thus no ancient records; what is known of their distant past comes from their enemies: The Chinese knew of them as far back as 1300 B.C. and faced a major Turkish invasion in the second century B.C. Their mobility and restlessness enabled the Turco-Turanian warriors to cover vast distances, from China to eastern Europe (they eventually attacked Vienna). Their mobility and restlessness was also accompanied by an openness of mind and a democratic view of life. They imported Nestorian Christianity and Persian fire-worship into China, and later, Islam to Europe. They carried Chinese silk to Byzantium; this trade involved them in treaties with Byzantium and Ethiopia at the time of Muhammad's birth and in a war with Persia. So far-reaching were their caravans that the oldest Buddhist temple in Japan contains Persian objects carried across Asia by Turkish traders.

In their democratic views they absorbed whatever people, whatever ideas or cultures, suited them, taking over customs, practices, religions, and even languages, for a "Turk" might from birth be a speaker of Persian, Chinese, or some other tongue rather than his ancestral Turkish. Rootless, ferocious in battle, they were as likely to attack relatives and friends as neighbors and strangers. National or racial consciousness did not exist: Instead they would crystallize around a magnetic leader, whose charismatic qualities, power, and fierce appetite for battle could dominate them and inspire future generations.

The special character of the Turks fascinated other peoples; the Arabs watched them uneasily as they approached. The historian al-Mas'udi described them thus:

> Those of them who are farthest to the north are the most subject to stupidity, grossness, and brutishness. The farther north, the more this is so. Such are those Turks who penetrate to the north. Because of their distance from the cir-

cuit of the sun when it rises and sets, there is much snow among them, and cold and damp have conquered their habitations; their bodies are slack and thick, and their backbones and neckbones so supple that they can shoot their arrows as they turn and flee. Their joints form hollows because they have so much flesh; their faces are round and their eyes small because the warmth concentrates in their faces while the cold takes possession of their bodies. The cold humor produces much blood; then their coloring grows red, since it is a quality of coldness to gather warmth and make it appear outside.

Considering the abysmal climate on the steppes it is no wonder the Turks sought warmer and richer lands. The warrior bands of Turks themselves were not large, but they aggregated hordes of the tribes they had conquered or overrun—warriors, women and children, artisans, slaves, and even beggars. But in their far-flung raids Turks themselves had also been taken prisoner and made slaves. Many of the Persians, among them the Sassanids and the Arsacids, and also the various khalifs had Turkish slaves in their courts. They became especially powerful at Baghdad, where the Abbasids had employed them as bodyguards, only to find that the slaves had, in effect, become the masters. They blackmailed the khalifs with threats, forcing them to take on kinsmen of the guards. Some of those Turks became so powerful that they attained high positions as governors or generals.

Border wars eventually turned into a full invasion. In the tenth century a group of Turks, later called the Seljuks (after the founder of their dynasty), threatened Afghanistan and Persia, and beyond them, Mesopotamia. Their leader was a minor warrior king named Yabgu. His chief general, a man named Tuqaq (the name means "Iron Bow"), described in an

Arab chronicle as a "man of resource, discernment, and competence," opposed the invasion for practical reasons. In the argument that followed, Tuqaq went too far and slapped the king's face, a most terrible insult, even for the democratic Turks. Yabgu had Tuqaq seized and bound, but eventually released him and did not follow up the invasion plan. When Tuqaq died not long after the incident, the king, who did not seem to harbor resentments, made his general's son, Seljuk ibn Tuqaq, still a teen-ager, commander of the army. The chronicle tells what happened next.

> The wife of the king of the Turks [Yabgu] used to make her husband fear the Amir Seljuk ibn Tuqaq and prevented him from trusting him or being at ease with him. This woman did not hide herself from him. One day she said to her husband, "Kingship is barren and cannot bear partnership. You will not savor the wine of kingship unless Seljuk is killed, and the dawn of your dominion will not shine unless you let him taste the cup of death. For soon he will trouble you and your realm and strive for your destruction." This was said within the sight and hearing of Amir Seljuk. Thereupon the Amir Seljuk went with his horses and soldiers to the land of Islam and was vouchsafed the bliss of the true religion. Choosing the neighborhood of Jand he drove out the infidel rulers and established himself there. Amir Seljuk lived for a hundred years. One night in a dream he saw himself ejaculate a fire, the sparks of which reached to the east and to the west. He asked an interpreter of dreams, who said, "From your seed kings will be born who will rule to the farthest ends of the world."

The prophecy indeed proved true. The Seljuk Turks soon overran parts of Afghanistan. One of the Seljuks, a man named Mahmud of Ghazni (after a town in Afghanistan), conquered

 The Crusades brought an entirely new kind of invader to the Middle East. Here Muslim warriors defend the key city of Tyre against attacking Christian armies. The city, which saw many battles, was taken by the Crusader Baldwin II in 1124. Both Christians and Muslims suffered from terrible divisions within their own ranks; eventually the Muslims, under the brilliant leader Saladin, regained most of the lost territory, though Crusader armies tried for years to retain a precarious foothold in the Middle East, valuable not only as the Holy Land but for its inestimable riches.

the Punjab area of western India, the same province which had once been invaded by Alexander the Great; this branch of the Seljuks was henceforth known as the Ghaznavids. Now the Turks fought among themselves. In 1040 the Seljuks defeated their Ghaznavid cousins and took over most of Iran. Fifteen years later the Seljuk prince Tughrul, having conquered everything left in Afghanistan and Iran, descended with his armies into Mesopotamia, and without much opposition rode with his troops up to the gates of Baghdad. The defenders fled, leaving the khalif, al-Kaim, no choice but to welcome his new master. Tughrul made the most of his conquest. He had himself invested as regent of the empire, king of the east and of the west, and took the title of sultan, meaning that he, and not the khalif, as in the past, was the supreme political and military authority. The khalif had to prostrate himself before the sultan and swear undying friendship and loyalty. After that the sultan abandoned Baghdad to his puppet khalif and retired to the more pleasant surroundings of Persia, where he did the khalifate the honor of marrying al-Kaim's daughter.

Again we need not entertain a recounting of every invader, every ruler, every decaying khalif in Mesopotamia. The great empire had long since broken up into separate kingdoms and khalifates; Egypt was the most important. More Turks came, and the Europeans, under the guise of saving Jerusalem from the Turks, proclaimed the Holy War in 1095, invaded the East, and temporarily freed the Holy City but became bogged down in a frightful morass, in which the Western knights slaughtered Eastern Christians as well as Muslims. The anti-crusades, as the Muslims called them, were fought by people other than the Mesopotamians. Most of the Islamic forces were composed of Turks or Kurds (one of the latter was the famous warrior Saladin), or Egyptians. The declining powers of Mesopotamia were not eager to enter into one more costly, endless state of warfare, in which they could only lose. The Crusades dragged on, both sides suffering. Mesopotamia and the Middle East soon faced another ferocious, unsparing enemy. This time it was the people who were cousins of the Turks, if not merely Turks under another name—the Mongols. The great Genghis Khan swept down from the steppes into Turkistan. The renowned old cities, jewels of this part of the world, Bukhara, Samarkand, and Balkh, great centers of commerce and learning, were captured by 1219 and reduced to ashes. Palaces, mosques, universities and schools, the libraries, the homes of private citizens, and the markets were razed to the ground and people slaughtered by the tens of thousands. Genghis Khan did not attack Mesopotamia, but his grandson Hulagu, who declared himself independent of the khans of the East, invaded Iran and marched on Iraq. Hulagu sent word to the current khalif, al-Musta'sim, to surrender. The khalif tried to equivocate, offering an evasive answer, but he could not argue his opponent into staying away from Baghdad. Soon the Mongols' artillery was poised before the city. Still the khalif could not believe that the enemy was about to attack, for he was "a man of poor judgment, irresolute and neglectful of what is needful for the conduct of government." His generals had told him that he ought either to propitiate the Mongols, submit, or fight, but his response had been that "Baghdad is good enough for me, and they will not begrudge it if I renounce all the other countries to them. Nor will they attack me when I am in it, for it is my house and residence." An Arab of a later generation, who recorded the fall of Baghdad, noted that al-Musta'sim was "devoted to entertainment and pleasure, passionately addicted to playing with birds, and dominated by women."

I present these details about the khalif because he was the last of the Abbasids, dying with his city in 1258. A man named Ibn Kathir gives what is almost a journalistic report of Baghdad's end, some of which reads like a modern newsweekly's account of the fall of a city.

> The Tatars [Mongols] surrounded the seat of the Khalifate and rained arrows on it from every side until a slave-girl was hit while she was playing before the Khalif and amusing him. She was one of his concubines, a mulatto called 'Urfa, and an arrow came through one of the windows and killed her while she was dancing before the Khalif. The Khalif was alarmed and very frightened.
>
> Hulagu Khan . . . came to Baghdad with his numerous infidel, profligate, tyrannical, brutal armies of men, who believed neither in God nor in the Last Day. . . . The armies of Baghdad were very few and utterly wretched, not reaching 10,000 horsemen [as opposed to the Mongols' 200,000 men]. They and the rest of the army had been deprived of their fiefs so that many of them were begging in the markets and by the gates of the mosques. Poets were reciting elegies on them and mourning for Islam and its people.

The khalif tried to buy off Hulagu Khan with jewels, but—

> The Tatars came down upon the city and killed all they could, men, women and children, the old, the middle-aged, and the young. Many of the people went into wells, latrines, and sewers and hid there for many days without emerging. Most of the people gathered in the caravanserais and locked themselves in. The Tatars opened the gates by either breaking or burning them. When they entered, the people in them fled upstairs and the Tatars killed them on the roofs until blood poured from the gutters into the streets. . . . The same happened in the mosques and the cathedral mosques

and the dervish convents. . . . And Baghdad, which had been the most civilized of all cities, became a ruin with only a few inhabitants, and they were in fear and hunger and wretchedness and insignificance.

Over a million people were massacred by the Mongols, including the khalif and his women. A few people were spared— the Christians and the Jews; Hulagu's wife was a Christian, and he had made a pact with the king of Armenia, a Byzantine Christian, that if he would spare all Christians and help regain Jerusalem for the Church, the Christians would help him in his war against the Muslims. But the pact was never realized. It was the Turks who drove the Mongols out after much heavy warfare, and it was other Turks who ousted the Seljuks, who had by now taken over the decrepit ruins of the Byzantine empire. The new Turks were the Osmanlis, or Ottomans, named after a great warrior, a ruthless aggressive leader named Othman. These people had been called in toward the end of the thirteenth century by the Seljuks to help drive off bands of Mongol marauders. There were only four hundred Osmanli families, and they were given a few hundred acres of land in southern Turkey by the Seljuks in return for their services against the Mongols. But again history repeats itself: Soon they had driven out some Greek garrisons on the northwest and had begun to conquer other parts of Turkey. The Seljuks, now a tottering dynasty, could not resist, and the Ottomans quickly had the entire area to themselves. They had taken over the most fertile areas of Anatolia. They turned their eyes westward, leaving Mesopotamia and Syria to other, less powerful tribes, these lands now disintegrating into provincial backwaters. The Ottomans reached the lower Danube in 1366 and defeated the French king, Louis of Anjou, who was lucky to escape with his life. Europe now became alarmed and desperately raised forces, but the next century was bleak for the Europeans. Muhammad II, the Conqueror, captured Constantinople in 1453, and Western and Christian rule in Asia was ended.

The very word "Turk" became awe-inspiring and frightening; they were thought invincible in battle. They held North Africa, part of Hungary and all of the Balkans, Anatolia and Cappadocia, all of Palestine and Mesopotamia and Iran, Afghanistan, western and northern India, and huge stretches of Asia into China. Even today, as the result of these Turkish conquests, a Turkish-speaking person can go from European Turkey across Asia almost to the Pacific speaking but his own language and its dialects.

Europe, split by rivalries, could not muster 40,000 troops against the Turks. The Turkish armies marched everywhere, making new conquests and putting down rebellions. They had the latest weapons, using large-bore cannons before any other nation. Certain routes were always followed by the army, for along them were the sources of supply. The Hungarian historian Julius Germanus describes the army on the march.

The army started on a campaign accompanied by an immense retinue of caterers, workmen, singers, and jugglers. The camp of a Turkish army presented the most picturesque sight imaginable. Races and costumes from all parts of the world, the whole bazaar of an Eastern town with its manifold products and entertainments, marched along with the fighters. The East marched up and down to Vienna across the Balkans a number of times.

The whole army, in contradistinction to those of other nations, had its peculiar uniform with gaudy colors; close fighting did not necessitate the dissimulation of khaki. Headgear played the most conspicuous part. Bulging trousers with different colored gaiters covering the calves, and heel-less high boots buttoned at their side made long and forced marches easy. While marching the wings of the overcoat were tucked into the belt to give the legs easier play.

The Turks' strength was in their military system: So long as they could conquer they were rich. But finance was the weakest part of the Ottoman empire. The soldiers could not balance the budget: Income and expenditures never matched. The palace expenses rose to uncontrollable heights. The provinces were looted and impoverished. Evil governors robbed the people and overtaxed and withheld income from the central government. The Ottoman empire, glued together out of the scattered fragments of old Sumer, Babylon, Greek, Roman, Persian, Arab, and Seljuk empires, plus a dozen or two of other conquests, became one of the worst of all places.

Until the time of Muhammad II the Conqueror, the Turkish sultan had been an openly seen, even fatherly, figure, dressed and living no differently from his warriors. But afterward, with the aggrandizement of lands and the new wealth of the conquered peoples, the sultan withdrew into the sacred confines of his palace and was rarely seen, being represented by his chief minister, the vezir (as the Turks spelled it). Needless to say, as Turkish initiative declined, the sultans became more and more reclusive, and the vezir more powerful. Within the palace and the harem murder, incest, and soft living reduced the position of sultan to a shadow.

The Ottoman empire began to distintegrate. But the Turks were able to retain Mesopotamia and Syria, provinces of a poverty so grinding that one could never imagine their early grandeur and wealth. Baghdad, as the chronicler of its last khalif had stated, remained a virtual ruin, its people existing in "fear and hunger and wretchedness and insignificance." Con-

 Today the young people of Mesopotamia and the Fertile Crescent are growing up in a new world. Oil, thermal energy, newly irrigated land, education, modern communications—all add up to give them wealth and opportunities denied their ancestors in the strife-torn past.

stantinople remained the center of rule. The Fertile Crescent degenerated into unappealing provinces at the mercy of unscrupulous Ottoman governors, whose main interest was in squeezing the last dinar, the last drachma, out of the wretched people. In the eighteenth and nineteenth centuries the European adventurers who searched the ancient tells could speak only of the misery of the populace and the corruption of the local pashas. Ottoman rule, once so dynamic, came, after five centuries, to be rule from the confines of the harem, where the sultans spent most of their time, refusing even to speak to cabinet ministers face to face, holding audiences from behind a screen and trying to avoid the day-to-day cares of the empire. Before the advent of World War I, which broke out in 1914, the Western powers could speak of Turkey as the "sick man of Europe." By that time the country was heavily infiltrated with German "advisers" (some of whom posed as archaeologists interested in the ancient mounds), who were subtly preparing to lay the groundwork for the exploitation of the empire's resources on behalf of the kaiser.

But the war, which brought the collapse of the Turks, also resulted in freedom for the old lands of Mesopotamia. France and England divided the provinces into "spheres of influence," but faraway rule could only be temporary by its nature. Syria did not achieve complete independence until 1944, but in 1921 Iraq—Sumer and Babylonia—was given an Arab ruler, Emir Faisal, formerly the king of Hejaz. Faisal II was assassinated in 1958, and a revolutionary party took over. A series of coups followed at five-year intervals, various groups of generals overthrowing and executing predecessors. But today Iraq is independent, and Baghdad, though not the great city of Harun al-Rashid, is a capital again.

INDEX